Words to Learn By

ADVANCING Academic Vocabulary

Stephen Dolainski • S. Elizabeth Griffin

DESPITE   ASPECT   BIAS

DISTINCTION

NEVERTHELESS

IMPLICATION

CRITERIA   PERSPECTIVE

ESTABLISH

INFER

McGraw Hill Education

Bothell, WA • Chicago, IL • Columbus, OH • New York, NY

Authors: Stephen Dolainski and Elizabeth Griffin

Stephen Dolainski is an adult educator, editor, and author. He has worked with the Los Angeles Unified School District for 18 years. As the Adult Basic Education Program adviser, Stephen supports teachers in classrooms across the district. He participated in the federal STAR initiative in California, and he completed training in evidence-based adult reading instruction. Now he trains other teachers to use evidence-based instruction in their classrooms. As an instructor, he has taught English as a Second Language (ESL), Adult Secondary Education, and Adult Basic Education (ABE). He is the author of *Grammar Traps: A Handbook of the 20 Most Common Grammar Mistakes and How to Avoid Them,* and he has contributed to numerous publications.

S. Elizabeth Griffin is an adult educator and teacher trainer. She has worked with a wide variety of students in a number of different programs from Peace Corps to Refugee Projects to Community Adult Schools. For almost 30 years, she has worked with students and teachers in the Los Angeles area. As an Adult Basic Education adviser for Los Angeles Unified School District, she participated in the federal STAR initiative in California and attended STAR trainings to deliver evidence-based adult reading instruction. She has trained adult education teachers and parole program teachers in evidence-based reading instruction. During her career, she has taught ESL, ABE, and Adult High-School-GED students. She currently works as a private consultant and trainer.

---

www.mheonline.com

 **Education**

Printed in the United States of America.

Send all inquiries to:
Contemporary/McGraw-Hill
130 East Randolph Street, Suite 400
Chicago, IL 60601

ISBN   978-0-07-658634-9
MHID   0-07-658634-0

3 4 5 6 7 8 9 QDB 15 14 13 12 11

The McGraw-Hill Companies

Contents

To the Student

Vocabulary is a key that unlocks meaning and comprehension. It opens doors to new ideas because it helps you become a better reader, writer, and student.

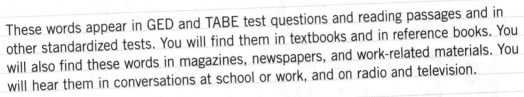

In **Words to Learn By: Advancing Academic Vocabulary,** you will learn 100 words. These words were carefully chosen for you. They are high-frequency academic words, which means you will find these words everywhere.

These words appear in GED and TABE test questions and reading passages and in other standardized tests. You will find them in textbooks and in reference books. You will also find these words in magazines, newspapers, and work-related materials. You will hear them in conversations at school or work, and on radio and television.

By learning these words, you will become a more successful student. These words will help you no matter what you are reading. They will also help you in classroom discussions and in your writing.

How to Use the Book

Words to Learn By: Advancing Academic Vocabulary has five units. Each unit includes four lessons in which you will learn five high-frequency words. First, the teacher will explain the meaning of each word and give examples. Then you will practice using the words.

It is important to use these words when you are not in class. Use them when you talk to friends and people at work. Listen for the words in conversations and on radio and television. If you are a parent, use the words with your children.

We believe that **Words to Learn By: Advancing Academic Vocabulary** will help you reach your academic goals. We wish you much success!

Stephen Dolainski and Elizabeth Griffin

according to

crucial

factor

perspective

exist

infer

isolated

priority

conclude

reasonable

incident

rationale

affect

encounter

exclude

consist

typical

qualify

restrict

criteria

conclude rationale affect according to
crucial reasonable exist **criteria** exclude
incident **perspective** encounter rationale
restrict factor isolated conclude **qualify**
consist priority **reasonable** typical infer

Vocabulary Knowledge Rating Chart

How well do you know the words? Use the numbers to rate your knowledge of the vocabulary words. Follow the teacher's directions.

4 = I know the word. I know it well enough to teach it to someone else.
3 = The word is familiar. I think I know what it means.
2 = I have heard the word, but I'm not sure what it means.
1 = I don't know the word at all.

	My rating before instruction	I think the word means	My rating after instruction
conclude			
criteria			
perspective			
qualify			
reasonable			

Word Meaning Chart

Complete the chart. Follow the teacher's directions.

conclude *(verb)* /kuhn KLOOD/

To **conclude** is to make a decision or judgment after considering information.

EXAMPLES

After reviewing the evidence, the detective _____ that two people were involved in the robbery.

Class Example: _____

My Example: After watching the instant replay, we **concluded** that _____

criteria *(noun)* /krahy TEER ee uh/

Criteria are things used to make a decision or judgment.

EXAMPLES

Before applying for the scholarship, it is important to know if you meet the _____.

Class Example: _____

My Example: I use a set of **criteria** when _____

perspective *(noun)* /per SPEK tiv/

Perspective is a particular way of thinking about something.

EXAMPLES

Students and teachers often have different _____ on homework.

Class Example: _____

My Example: From the **perspective** of children, adults _____

qualify *(verb)* /KWOL uh fahy/

To **qualify** means to meet necessary requirements or conditions to do or receive something.

EXAMPLES

The Gomezes were pleased to learn that they _____ for the car loan.

Class Example: _____

My Example: Being a citizen **qualifies** a person to _____

reasonable *(adjective)* /REE zuh nuh buhl/

Reasonable tells that something is fair, appropriate, or makes sense.

EXAMPLES

Good public transportation is reliable with _____ wait times.

Class Example: _____

My Example: A **reasonable** amount of time to walk one mile is _____

Exercise 1 Use the Words

Complete each sentence. Write the correct form of the vocabulary word in the blank space.

1. The story was told from the _____ of a Confederate soldier during the Civil War.

2. What _____ are important to you when you vote for a candidate?

3. Sergio has worked at his job for less than six months, so he does not

   _____ for unemployment benefits.

4. Tina's explanation that the dog ate her homework was not _____.

5. The doctor _____ that Mrs. Johnston's rash was an allergic reaction.

Exercise 2 Complete the Sentences

These sentences have been started for you. They are not complete. Complete them with your own words.

1. It is reasonable to expect a teacher to _____

   _____

   _____

2. One of my criteria for buying a car is _____

   _____

   _____

3. I did not qualify for the job because _____

   _____

   _____

4. After reading the job description, I concluded _____

   _____

   _____

5. Compared to my parents, I have a different perspective on _____

   _____

   _____

Words at Work

Circle the best answer to each multiple choice question below. Then write a brief response to the question that follows. Write your answers in complete sentences.

1. Marsha has completed her first year with the company. As a result, she qualifies for a 5 percent pay raise. What does this mean for Marsha?

   (A) She will wait to make more money.
   (B) She will make more money now.
   (C) She will make more money next year.

   What is something else that can qualify an employee for a raise? _____

   _____

2. Home Hardware is a large company with many employees. Each month, an outstanding employee receives the Employee of the Month award. What is one of the criteria for this award?

   (A) The award is given once a month.
   (B) The employee has an excellent attendance record.
   (C) The store creates a positive atmosphere.

   What do you think are other criteria for this award? _____

   _____

3. Stan needs to adjust his work schedule in order to pick up his children after school two days each week. What is a reasonable request he can make to his manager?

   (A) ask to leave one hour earlier
   (B) ask to come in one hour earlier and leave one hour earlier
   (C) ask to come in one hour later and leave one hour earlier

   What is another reasonable need that people have for requesting a schedule change?

   _____

   _____

4. S&E Designs asked its employees to park in the back of the lot to provide customer parking near the entrance. They also asked employees to greet customers and to offer to carry boxes to their cars. What is reasonable for the employees to conclude about their employer? The company is

   (A) not interested in employees' needs.
   (B) not interested in customers' needs.
   (C) interested in customers' needs.

   What else can you conclude about the company? _____

   _____

Word Families

Most words are part of a family of words. Study the word families on this page. Then fill in the missing words using the correct form of each word.

---

conclude *(verb)*

- conclusion *(noun)*
  The city council came to the conclusion that the city needed more stoplights.

reasonable *(adjective)*

- reasonably *(adverb)*
  My grandmother was in reasonably good health until she was 90.

qualify *(verb)*

- qualification *(noun)*
  Being a strong swimmer is one of the qualifications to be a lifeguard.

- qualified *(adjective)*
  After five years at the restaurant, Walter was well qualified to be a manager.

---

1. Many soccer teams do not _____ for the World Cup tournament.

2. Are you _____ satisfied with your new apartment?

3. Make sure you have a _____ plumber install your new shower.

4. After reviewing the budget, Don reached the _____ that he could not afford a new car.

5. Jamal has all the _____ for the position except the required experience.

Complete the paragraph using the correct forms of the five vocabulary words in this lesson. Each form of a word is used only once.

Qualifications for President

Who is _____ to be president of the United States? A person has
                    6.

the minimum _____ if he or she is at least 35 years old, was born
                    7.

in the U.S., and has lived in the country for at least 14 years. Voters must consider other

_____. For example, a candidate should be _____
          8.   9.

intelligent and able to draw _____ to make critical decisions. The person
                        10.

needs to understand the different _____ of average Americans. Although
                              11.

many people may _____ for the position, it is _____
                  12.   13.

to _____ that very few will actually run for office.
      14.

Coaches and athletes should share the same perspective on what it takes to win.

Exercise 5 What Do You Think?

Read each question and write a brief answer. Explain your answers in complete sentences.

1. Is it reasonable to conclude that a person who is a good athlete also qualifies as a good coach?

_____

_____

_____

2. Is being able to speak English a reasonable qualification for a job?

_____

_____

_____

3. From your perspective, would you conclude that money is more valuable than time?

_____

_____

_____

The American Jury System

The American jury system is one of the most respected legal systems in the world. A jury is a group of citizens that listens to the evidence presented in a courtroom during a trial. A jury then determines guilt or innocence.

The concept of a jury trial is very old, dating back to ancient Greece. Because the United States began as colonies of Britain, the American system is based on the British model. An American jury is made up of twelve average citizens called jurors.

To be a juror, a person must be at least 18 years old, a U.S. citizen, and able to speak English. Potential jurors are selected from lists of registered voters, licensed drivers, and other sources. The judge and lawyers ask the potential jurors questions to learn if they are able to make a fair decision based on the law.

During a trial, the jurors listen to the evidence presented by lawyers and testimony from witnesses from both sides. The jurors are not allowed to talk about the case with anyone for the duration of the trial. The judge explains the particular laws that apply to the case. The jurors discuss the case and reach a verdict—guilt or innocence.

A jury trial is one way to prevent the government from having too much power. In a jury trial, the people, not the government, decide who is guilty and who is innocent. This fundamental right is guaranteed by the U.S. Constitution and the constitutions of each of the fifty states.

Being a juror is one of the most important civic duties a U.S. citizen can perform.

1. What criteria must a person meet in order to qualify as a potential juror?

_____

_____

_____

2. From the perspective of a juror, what could be a possible challenge?

_____

_____

_____

3. What happens in a trial before the jury comes to its conclusion about guilt or innocence?

_____

_____

_____

conclude rationale affect according to
crucial reasonable exist **criteria** exclude
incident **perspective** encounter rationale
restrict factor isolated conclude **qualify**
consist priority **reasonable** typical infer

New Word List

☐ conclude

☐ criteria

☐ perspective

☐ qualify

☐ reasonable

Exercise 7 # Writing Connection

Write a brief response to each question. Use words from this lesson in your answer. Write your answers in complete sentences.

"You never truly know someone until you have walked a mile in his or her shoes." How does knowing the perspective of another person help you understand that person? Refer to the quote and use an example to explain your answer.

_____

_____

_____

_____

_____

Imagine you are writing a job description for a parent. What are the minimum criteria? What should qualify a person to be a parent?

_____

_____

_____

_____

_____

_____

Exercise 8 # Reflection

Think about the words you have studied in this lesson.

1. Which words did you enjoy learning? _____

2. Select one word and imagine where you will use the word. Explain the situation.

_____

_____

3. Which words do you still need help with? _____

4. Return to the Knowledge Rating Chart at the beginning of this lesson. Complete column 3. How have your responses changed?

affect conclude **according to** consist
crucial reasonable criteria exclude exist
incident perspective rationale **encounter**
restrict **factor** isolated conclude qualify
rationale priority typical **infer** reasonable

Vocabulary Knowledge Rating Chart

How well do you know the words? Use the numbers to rate your knowledge of the vocabulary words. Follow the teacher's directions.

4 = I know the word. I know it well enough to teach it to someone else.
3 = The word is familiar. I think I know what it means.
2 = I have heard the word, but I'm not sure what it means.
1 = I don't know the word at all.

	My rating before instruction	I think the word means	My rating after instruction
according to			
crucial			
encounter			
factor			
infer			

Word Meaning Chart

Complete the chart. Follow the teacher's directions.

according to *(preposition)* /uh KAWR ding/

According to means that something is based on what has been said or reported.

EXAMPLES

The economy, _____ the president, has improved since last year.

Class Example: _____

My Example: **According to** the weather report, _____

crucial *(adjective)* /KROO shuhl/

Crucial tells that something is extremely important and may determine success or failure.

EXAMPLES

It was _____ for Linda to get new tires before driving cross-country.

Class Example: _____

My Example: The doctor made a **crucial** decision to _____

encounter *(verb)* /en KOUN ter/

Encounter means to meet someone or something, usually unexpectedly.

EXAMPLES

When the father suggested moving, he _____ opposition from the entire family.

Class Example: _____

My Example: I **encountered** great difficulty when _____

factor *(noun)* /FAK ter/

A **factor** is something that contributes to a result.

EXAMPLES

The weather was a major _____ in the cancellation of flights for the day.

Class Example: _____

My Example: One **factor** in a person's decision to change jobs is _____

infer *(verb)* /in FUR/

To **infer** is to connect new information with previously known information to form an idea or judgment.

EXAMPLES

Based on the evidence, the detective _____ that the criminal was a woman.

Class Example: _____

My Example: I might **infer** that a person is not a good driver if _____

Exercise 1 Use the Words

Complete each sentence. Write the correct form of the vocabulary word in the blank space.

1. Why are vaccinations _____ for young children's health?

2. A fire truck and two ambulances passed me on their way to the accident scene.

   I _____ that many people were critically injured.

3. The hikers were surprised to _____ a large snake on the trail.

4. _____ statistics, people with a diploma earn more money than those without one.

5. The rise in gas prices was one _____ in the increase in the cost of postage.

Exercise 2 Complete the Sentences

These sentences have been started for you. They are not complete. Complete them with your own words.

1. I can infer that my new neighbors will be good ones because _____

   _____

   _____

2. A time that I encountered a helpful person was when _____

   _____

   _____

3. According to my grandparents, _____

   _____

   _____

4. One necessary factor in a team's success is _____

   _____

   _____

5. A crucial issue for our country now is _____

   _____

   _____

Words at Work

Circle the best answer to each multiple choice question below. Then write a brief response to the question that follows. Write your answers in complete sentences.

1. Carl and his coworkers usually wear jeans and t-shirts to work. Today, however, Carl came to work in a shirt and tie. He also asked for permission to take an extra hour for lunch. What might his coworkers infer about Carl?

   (A) He bought new clothes.   **(B)** He has a job interview.   **(C)** He wants a pay raise.

   What is something else you might infer about Carl? _____

   _____

   _____

2. The city newspaper published an article about the Redbird Café. The reporter spoke to several people who had eaten there. She wrote that the food was delicious and the service was excellent. This was according to

   (A) the customers.   **(B)** the cooks.   **(C)** the servers.

   According to the owners, all the breads and soups at Redbird Café are homemade. What is a comment you might read from the perspective of an employee?

   _____

   _____

3. During Sally's first week on the job, she encountered several challenges. What was one of them?

   (A) her attitude   **(B)** her inability to use new   **(C)** her willingness to clean her
                                      machinery effectively   work area

   What is another challenge a new employee might encounter? _____

   _____

   _____

4. There are many factors in having a successful job interview. One crucial factor is

   (A) arriving very early.   **(B)** wearing stylish clothes.   **(C)** arriving on time.

   What is another crucial factor? _____

   _____

   _____

Exercise 4 Word Families

Most words are part of a family of words. Study the word families on this page. Then fill in the missing words using the correct form of each word.

---

encounter *(verb)*

- encounter *(noun)*
  Tanya likes her job despite occasional encounters with rude customers.

infer *(verb)*

- inference *(noun)*
  Members of a jury make inferences after listening to witnesses.

factor *(noun)*

- factor in *(verb)*
  You have to factor in sales tax when you add up all the costs of new furniture.
- factor out *(verb)*
  Net income is the money you earn after you factor out taxes and deductions.

---

1. It is essential to make a child's first _____ with a dentist a positive one.

2. What _____ can you draw from the information presented in the graph?

3. After she _____ her time, Marta concluded that it was cheaper to buy cakes for the party than to make them.

4. Because of Tony's behavior, the teacher _____ that he had stayed up all night studying.

5. My workday is seven hours after I _____ an hour for lunch and breaks.

Complete the paragraph using the correct forms of the five vocabulary words in this lesson. Each form of a word is used only once.

Cholesterol

The liver produces cholesterol which is _____ for keeping cells healthy.
                                              6.
However, too much cholesterol can be dangerous. It often _____ as a
                                                                7.
major cause of heart attacks and other heart problems. _____ research, it
                                                              8.
is important to control the amount of cholesterol in your body. Two _____
                                                                        9.
in controlling cholesterol are exercise and diet. Therefore, if you _____
                                                                        10.
someone who exercises regularly and eats a low-fat diet, you could _____
                                                                        11.
that he or she has a healthy heart.

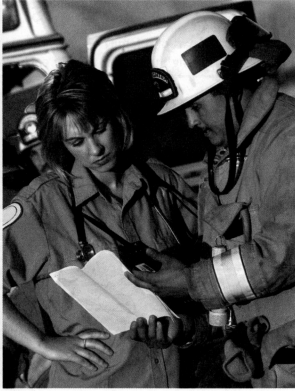

Police and paramedics make crucial decisions every day.

Exercise 5 What Do You Think?

Read each question and write a brief answer. Explain your answers in complete sentences.

1. Which job requires a person to make more crucial inferences: a police officer or a paramedic?

_____

_____

_____

2. Can you infer that a person is wealthy or poor according to the way he or she is dressed?

_____

_____

_____

3. Which is a more crucial experience in life: an encounter with danger or an encounter with love?

_____

_____

Reading Connection

Read the following passage. Answer the questions using complete sentences.

How Long Will You Live?

Jeanne Calment was born in 1875 in France. She died in 1997 at the age of 122. She lived longer than any other human being.

What factors contributed to Jeanne Calment's very long life? Scientists believe that genes are a major factor in how long people live. Genes can be passed on from one generation to another. Jeanne's parents lived long lives too. Her father lived to be 94, and her mother died at 86. Many of her relatives lived into their 80s.

Other factors influence how long a person lives. Gender, for example, may play a part in a person's life expectancy. Women may live longer than men do in some areas of the world. Diet and exercise are important too. Smoking and drug use can shorten a person's life. Disease and war also impact life expectancy.

One significant factor is the quality of life in the country where a person is born. People may live longer in the wealthier areas of Europe, North America, and Asia where the quality of life is higher. People in poorer places with a lower quality of life, however, may not live as long.

The chart on the right lists the average life expectancy of people in 12 countries around the world.

Country	Continent	Life Expectancy
Afghanistan	Asia	45
Angola	Africa	38
Brazil	S. America	72
Canada	N. America	81
China	Asia	73
Japan	Asia	82
Kenya	Africa	58
Mexico	N. America	76
Niger	Africa	52
Russia	Europe/Asia	66
Spain	Europe	80
United States	N. America	78

1. What factors enable a person to live a long life?

_____

_____

2. According to the chart, what can you infer about the quality of life in Afghanistan?

_____

_____

_____

3. What choices do people make that may be crucial to their life expectancy?

_____

_____

affect conclude **according to** consist
crucial reasonable criteria exclude exist
incident perspective rationale **encounter**
restrict **factor** isolated conclude quality
rationale priority typical **infer** reasonable

New Word List

☐ according to

☐ crucial

☐ encounter

☐ factor

☐ infer

Review Word List

☐ _____

☐ _____

☐ _____

☐ _____

☐ _____

Exercise 7 Writing Connection

Write a brief response to each question. Use words from this lesson or the previous lesson in your answer. Write your answers in complete sentences.

Who is or was a crucial person in your life? How was this person a factor in your success, growth, or development?

_____

_____

_____

_____

_____

Reflect on your first encounter with school. Describe it. What factors made it a negative or positive experience?

_____

_____

_____

_____

_____

_____

Exercise 8 Reflection

Think about the words you have studied in this lesson.

1. Which words did you enjoy learning? _____

2. Select one word and imagine where you will use the word. Explain the situation.

_____

_____

3. Which words do you still need help with? _____

4. Return to the Knowledge Rating Chart at the beginning of this lesson. Complete column 3. How have your responses changed?

affect conclude infer according to consist
crucial reasonable criteria **exclude** exist
incident **rationale** encounter perspective
qualify isolated conclude factor **restrict**
rationale priority **typical** reasonable infer

Vocabulary Knowledge Rating Chart

How well do you know the words? Use the numbers to rate your knowledge of the vocabulary words. Follow the teacher's directions.

4 = I know the word. I know it well enough to teach it to someone else.
3 = The word is familiar. I think I know what it means.
2 = I have heard the word, but I'm not sure what it means.
1 = I don't know the word at all.

	My rating before instruction	I think the word means	My rating after instruction
affect			
exclude			
rationale			
restrict			
typical			

Word Meaning Chart

Complete the chart. Follow the teacher's directions.

affect *(verb)* /uh FEKT/

To **affect** means to have an influence on or to cause a change in someone or something.

EXAMPLES

Asthma _____ a person's ability to breathe.

Class Example: _____

My Example: Being hungry **affects** my ability to _____

exclude *(verb)* /ik SKLOOD/

To **exclude** means to not allow or to not include someone or something.

EXAMPLES

Theme parks _____ small children from some rides for safety concerns.

Class Example: _____

My Example: A place that **excludes** pets is _____

rationale *(noun)* /rash uh NAL/

Rationale is the basis, or set of reasons, for deciding or doing something.

EXAMPLES

Reducing crime is a strong _____ for hiring more police officers.

Class Example: _____

My Example: My **rationale** for getting a diploma includes _____

restrict *(verb)* /ri STRIKT/

To **restrict** means to put limits on or to control someone or something.

EXAMPLES

The city _____ overnight parking on many of its streets.

Class Example: _____

My Example: Velma's diet **restricts** her to _____

typical *(adjective)* /TIP i kuhl/

Typical tells that something has qualities that are usual and expected or common.

EXAMPLES

A _____ young child does not like to share his or her toys.

Class Example: _____

My Example: A **typical** morning for me includes _____

Exercise 1   Use the Words

Complete each sentence. Write the correct form of the vocabulary word in the blank space.

1. What was Cyndi's _____ for moving to Chicago?

2. Coffee _____ Rahsaan. It keeps him awake at night.

3. Katie's snowboarding injury _____ her to a wheelchair for two months.

4. A _____ Thanksgiving dinner includes roasted turkey and stuffing.

5. Newspaper articles _____ the names of victims until their families are contacted.

Exercise 2   Complete the Sentences

These sentences have been started for you. They are not complete. Complete them with your own words.

1. A typical teenager enjoys _____

   _____

   _____

2. Regular exercise can affect _____

   _____

   _____

   _____

3. A way to protect the environment is to restrict _____

   _____

   _____

4. The need to improve test scores is a rationale for _____

   _____

   _____

5. The coach excluded Sam from the game because _____

   _____

   _____

Words at Work

Circle the best answer to each multiple choice question below. Then write a brief response to the question that follows. Write your answers in complete sentences.

---

1. On a typical work day, Santos starts his shift at 11:00 P.M. and finishes at 7:00 A.M. He usually takes a lunch break around 3:00 A.M. to have a bowl of soup or a sandwich. Why was today not a typical day for Santos?

   (A) He took his break at 3:05 A.M.

   (B) He started working at 11:00 P.M.

   (C) He worked until 7:30 A.M.

   What is a typical work or school day schedule for you? _____

   _____

2. Louisa's new job provides medical benefits. However, the benefits only include Louisa. They exclude dependents until Louisa has been employed with the company for two years. How does this affect Louisa's family?

   (A) She will pay for her doctor visits.

   (B) She will pay for her children's doctor visits.

   (C) She will not pay for her visits after two years.

   Why do you think a company would exclude an employee's dependents? _____

   _____

3. Smoking regulations at Western Life Insurance Company restrict smokers to certain outside areas. A diagram in the company handbook shows the areas. How do the regulations affect smokers?

   (A) They can smoke in certain parts of the building.

   (B) They can smoke anywhere outside the building.

   (C) They can only smoke in certain areas outside the building.

   What is another place that restricts smoking? _____

   _____

4. Lee told his family and friends that he has decided to move to another city. People were surprised, but they wished him luck because they thought he had a reasonable rationale for his decision. What was Lee's rationale?

   (A) He has never been to the new city.

   (B) He is having trouble finding a job where he lives now.

   (C) He is too old to live in the same city as his parents.

   What is another reasonable rationale for moving to another city or state? _____

   _____

Exercise 4 Word Families

Most words are part of a family of words. Study the word families on this page. Then fill in the missing words using the correct form of each word.

---

exclude *(verb)*

- exclusion *(noun)*
  The exclusion of women from voting ended in 1921.

- excluding *(preposition)*
  Concert tickets cost $30 each, excluding the service charge.

restrict *(verb)*

- restriction *(noun)*
  Our apartment complex has a restriction on loud music after 10 P.M.

- restricted *(adjective)*
  Some movies are restricted to people over 17.

typical *(adverb)*

- typically *(noun)*
  Girls typically mature earlier than boys do.

---

1. Skateboarding is _____ to a particular area in the park.

2. Throughout most of the country, summer afternoons are _____ hot and humid.

3. Airport police enforce parking _____ in front of all terminals.

4. Is the _____ of women from the military still common in most countries around the world?

5. The coupon was good for 15% off all items, _____ jewelry and watches.

Complete the paragraph using the correct forms of the five vocabulary words in this lesson. Each form of a word is used only once.

The Color Line

At one time, there were _____ on who could play baseball. Black
                                            6.

players were _____ from playing in the major leagues. There was no
                        7.

reasonable _____ for this segregation. It was based on prejudice. It
                    8.

_____ black players for 80 years. In 1946, Jackie Robinson became the
          9.

first black major league baseball player, and the _____ of black players
                                                              10.

ended. Baseball teams today are _____ made up of players of different
                                            11.

nationalities and races.

The Internet affects how families interact.

What Do You Think?

Read each question and write a brief answer. Explain your answers in complete sentences.

1. Would typical parents restrict their children to using the Internet only when an adult is present?

   _____

   _____

   _____

2. Is there a rationale for believing that the health issues of one person can affect everyone in society?

   _____

   _____

   _____

3. Is there ever a reasonable rationale to exclude a relative from an important family event like a wedding or funeral?

   _____

   _____

Reading Connection

Read the following passage. Answer the questions using complete sentences.

A World of Myths

Did you ever wonder what causes thunder and lightning? Or why volcanoes erupt with smoke and fire? Or why there is sickness and suffering in the world? Ancient people all over the world wondered about the same things. They did not have the benefit of science as we do today. Instead, they created stories to explain why there are earthquakes and why people fall in love.

These stories are called myths. Because myths explain things that humans cannot control or understand, the main characters in myths are gods, goddesses, and supernatural heroes.

In Hawaii, for example, there is a myth about Pele, the goddess of fire. The myth explains how Pele created Hawaii's volcanoes.

The ancient Greeks had a myth to explain why there are bad things like evil and disease in the world. Zeus, the king of the gods, sent his daughter Pandora to earth to get married. His wedding present was a big box with a lock on it. Zeus told Pandora never to open the box, but Pandora did not listen. When she opened the box, she released envy, crime, hate, disease, and other bad things into the world.

The ancient Romans liked the Greek gods and goddesses and adopted them for their own. However, they changed the names. Zeus became Jupiter. Zeus's wife, Hera, was changed to Juno. Aphrodite was the Greek goddess of beauty and love. The Romans renamed her Venus. Poseidon, the Greek god of the sea, got the name Neptune.

The Romans also gave us an explanation for love—an arrow shot into a heart by Cupid, the son of Venus.

1. A typical myth tells a story that involves a god or goddess. What is the rationale for these characters?

_____

_____

_____

2. Are myths restricted to ancient Greeks and Romans? Are you familiar with myths of other ancient peoples?

_____

_____

_____

3. How did myths affect ancient people? What can you infer about the ancient world?

_____

_____

affect conclude infer according to consist crucial reasonable criteria **exclude** exist incident **rationale** encounter perspective quality isolated conclude factor **restrict** rationale priority **typical** reasonable infer

New Word List

☐ affect

☐ exclude

☐ rationale

☐ restrict

☐ typical

Review Word List

☐ _____

☐ _____

☐ _____

☐ _____

☐ _____

Exercise 7 Writing Connection

Write a brief response to each question. Use words from this lesson or previous lessons in your answer. Write your answers in complete sentences.

If you were the governor of your state, is there a current restriction you would remove? Or is there one you would add? What would be your rationale? How would your decision affect people?

_____

_____

_____

_____

_____

Think about a crucial decision you made. Explain your rationale and identify the factors that affected your decision.

_____

_____

_____

_____

_____

Exercise 8 Reflection

Think about the words you have studied in this lesson.

1. Which words did you enjoy learning? _____

2. Select one word and imagine where you will use the word. Explain the situation.

_____

_____

3. Which words do you still need help with? _____

4. Return to the Knowledge Rating Chart at the beginning of this lesson. Complete column 3. How have your responses changed?

affect infer according to **consist** conclude
crucial reasonable criteria exclude **exist**
incident encounter perspective rationale
restrict factor conclude **isolated** qualify
rationale **priority** typical reasonable infer

Vocabulary Knowledge Rating Chart

How well do you know the words? Use the numbers to rate your knowledge of the vocabulary words. Follow the teacher's directions.

4 = I know the word. I know it well enough to teach it to someone else.
3 = The word is familiar. I think I know what it means.
2 = I have heard the word, but I'm not sure what it means.
1 = I don't know the word at all.

	My rating before instruction	I think the word means	My rating after instruction
consist			
exist			
incident			
isolated			
priority			

Word Meaning Chart

Complete the chart. Follow the teacher's directions.

---

consist *(verb)* /kuhn SIST/

To **consist** means to be made of or to include different parts or things.

EXAMPLES

A typical jury in a criminal trial _____ of 12 jurors and 2 alternates.

Class Example: _____

My Example: A vegetarian diet may **consist** of _____

---

exist *(verb)* /ig ZIST/

To **exist** means to be alive, real, or present in a place or situation.

EXAMPLES

The American Cancer Society _____ to raise money for cancer research.

Class Example: _____

My Example: Laws **exist** to _____

---

incident *(noun)* /IN si duhnt/

An **incident** is something that happens that is usually serious, unpleasant, or sometimes dangerous.

EXAMPLES

Although the _____ with the unfriendly dog happened many years ago, Reyna never forgot it.

Class Example: _____

My Example: The famous actor created an **incident** when _____

---

isolated *(adjective)* /AHY suh ley tid/

Isolated tells that someone or something is alone, separate, far away, or happening only once.

EXAMPLES

The argument after the game was an _____ disturbance. There are usually no problems.

Class Example: _____

My Example: The new student felt **isolated** because _____

---

priority *(noun)* /prahy AWR i tee/

A **priority** is the most important thing that needs attention before anything else.

EXAMPLES

Improving students' test scores is a _____ for teachers.

Class Example: _____

My Example: A **priority** for new parents is _____

Exercise 1   Use the Words

Complete each sentence. Write the correct form of the vocabulary word in the blank space.

1. A government official who disrespects a country's leader can create an international

 _____ .

2. The executive branch of government _____ of the president, the vice-president, and fifteen cabinet departments.

3. The new governor concluded that education would be his top _____ .

4. "I hope your high test scores are not _____ results," the teacher told Tom.

5. How long can a person _____ without food or water?

Exercise 2   Complete the Sentences

These sentences have been started for you. They are not complete. Complete them with your own words.

1. Every week, a priority for me is _____

 _____

 _____

2. A typical breakfast for me consists of _____

 _____

 _____

3. A person may want an isolated place when _____

 _____

 _____

4. Libraries exist for people to _____

 _____

 _____

5. The incident in the park occurred when _____

 _____

 _____

Words at Work

Circle the best answer to each multiple choice question below. Then write a brief response to the question that follows. Write your answers in complete sentences.

1. The company has set a priority to ship all orders on the day they are received. Alfredo is the shipping clerk. How does this priority affect Alfredo? He may have to

   (A) work overtime.   **(B)** take an extra break.   **(C)** leave work early.

   How else might this priority affect Alfredo? _____

   _____

2. Crystal has a new job as a cashier and receptionist at VZ Auto Body Shop. Her job consists mainly of answering phones and handling payments. According to this job description, Crystal will

   (A) call insurance   **(B)** take messages.   **(C)** order car parts.
   companies.

   What are other tasks that Crystal's job may consist of? _____

   _____

   _____

3. Jordan Taylor was extremely late for his shift today. His car broke down, and he had left his cell phone at home. His manager was very upset. Jordan apologized and assured the manager that his lateness was an isolated incident. What did Jordan say?

   (A) "I have a record of always   **(B)** "I was late only three   **(C)** "I only took a one-week
   being on time."   times last month."   vacation."

   Why should Jordan stress that his lateness was an isolated incident? _____

   _____

   _____

4. Latisha works at Felton Electronics, a store well known for its customer satisfaction guarantee. Latisha tells customers that this guarantee has existed since the store opened. Why do customers feel confident about shopping at Felton Electronics?

   (A) Similar guarantees exist   **(B)** A guarantee exists only   **(C)** A history of reliable
   at other stores.   when the store is open.   customer service exists.

   Do you prefer to shop at a store where a customer satisfaction guarantee exists? Why?

   _____

   _____

Word Families

Most words are part of a family of words. Study the word families on this page. Then fill in the missing words using the correct form of each word.

---

exist *(verb)*
• existence *(noun)*   *Most people do not believe in the existence of ghosts.*   • existing *(adjective)*   *The new rates do not apply to existing members, only new members.*

isolated *(adjective)*
• isolate *(verb)*   *Many celebrities try to isolate themselves and their children from reporters.*   • isolation *(noun)*   *Patients are kept in isolation to prevent potential infections.*

priority *(noun)*
• prioritize *(verb)*   *After making a list of tasks, it's important to prioritize them.*

1. The army general concluded that his plan to _____ the town was not successful.

2. "Why don't _____ customers qualify for the special offer?" the woman asked.

3. Gloria _____ her list of possible wedding dates before e-mailing the list to her family.

4. Before the _____ of cameras, people relied on drawings or paintings.

5. A hermit is a person who chooses to live in _____, far away from other people.

Complete the paragraph using the correct forms of the vocabulary words from this lesson. Each form of a word is used only once.

Alaska

Alaska is the largest and most _____ state in the U.S. It
                                              6.

_____ of mountains, glaciers, rivers, lakes, and islands. Preservation
            7.

of its natural beauty and wilderness areas is a _____. The largest
                                                              8.

_____ oil fields in North America are found in Alaska. An oil spill in
            9.

1989 created a serious environmental _____. Although cities and towns
                                                10.

_____, many Alaskans enjoy their _____.
            11.   **12.**

Does life exist on other planets?

Exercise 5 What Do You Think?

Read each question and write a brief answer. Explain your answers in complete sentences.

1. Should finding out if life exists on other planets be a priority for the government?

_____

_____

_____

2. Do isolated incidents of crime in a neighborhood provide a reasonable rationale to move?

_____

_____

_____

3. Should priority be given to a group of students that consists of top athletes or a group that consists of top students?

_____

_____

_____

Reading Connection

Read the following passage. Answer the questions using complete sentences.

Rachel Carson and *Silent Spring*

In 1962, the book *Silent Spring* was published. It had a crucial impact on America. The author, Rachel Carson, was a well-known biologist and writer.

Silent Spring told how chemicals used in pesticides affected the environment. One dangerous pesticide was called DDT. It was used to kill mosquitoes and other insects. Airplanes flew over large areas of the country spraying DDT on crops, rivers, and even people's houses. At the time, people believed there were many benefits of pesticides. They did not know about the dangers.

Rachel Carson studied the effects of DDT on the environment. According to the research, DDT was a crucial factor in health problems in wildlife. Some birds, for example, had difficulty reproducing because the shells of their eggs were too thin. The thin shells were because of DDT.

She also wrote that the companies that made pesticides did not fully inform the public of all the possible dangers. Moreover, she thought the government did not sufficiently challenge the companies to prove that the chemicals were safe.

She concluded, therefore, that there should be stronger regulations to restrict the use of pesticides. DDT, however, should be excluded completely because it was so dangerous.

Silent Spring sold more than 500,000 copies. President Kennedy formed a special committee to study the issues Rachel Carson wrote about in *Silent Spring*. Congress investigated the dangers of pesticides. Eventually, DDT was prohibited. Since then, other laws and regulations have restricted the use of chemicals in the environment.

Although Rachel Carson died in 1964 at the age of 57, she had planted the seeds for the modern environmental movement.

1. DDT consists of dangerous chemicals. According to Rachel Carson, what problems existed in the environment because of DDT?

   _____

   _____

2. Were the incidents that Rachel Carson wrote about in *Silent Spring* isolated in one part of the country?

   _____

   _____

3. How did *Silent Spring* make the environment a priority in America?

   _____

   _____

affect infer according to **consist** conclude
crucial reasonable criteria exclude **exist**
incident encounter perspective rationale
restrict factor conclude **isolated** qualify
rationale **priority** typical reasonable infer

New Word List

☐ consist

☐ exist

☐ incident

☐ isolated

☐ priority

Review Word List

☐ _____

☐ _____

☐ _____

☐ _____

☐ _____

Exercise 7 # Writing Connection

Write a brief response to each question. Use words from this lesson or previous lessons in your answer. Write your answers in complete sentences.

Describe an ideal birthday party. What does the menu consist of? Whom does the guest list consist of? Is there anyone you would exclude?

_____

_____

_____

_____

_____

Do you believe the existence of computers has increased or reduced isolation among people? Give specific examples to support your answer.

_____

_____

_____

_____

_____

Exercise 8 # Reflection

Think about the words you have studied in this lesson.

1. Which words did you enjoy learning? _____

2. Select one word and imagine where you will use the word. Explain the situation.

_____

_____

3. Which words do you still need help with? _____

4. Return to the Knowledge Rating Chart at the beginning of this lesson. Complete column 3. How have your responses changed?

Activity 1 ## Ask Questions

Look at the picture of workers cleaning a beach after an oil spill. Imagine you have the opportunity to ask the oil company about the oil spill and the clean up. Write at least five questions you want to ask the oil company officials. Use one or more of the vocabulary words you have studied in this unit in each question. <u>Underline</u> each vocabulary word you use. Some of your questions can begin with *Who, What, When, Where, Why,* or *How*.

Examples: From the company's <u>perspective</u>, what is a <u>reasonable</u> amount of time to complete the clean up?
Will this <u>incident</u> <u>restrict</u> your ability to drill for more oil?

_____

_____

_____

_____

_____

_____

_____

_____

_____

_____

WORD BANK

ACCORDING
AFFECT
CONCLUDE
CONSIST
CRITERIA
CRUCIAL
ENCOUNTER
EXCLUDE
EXIST
FACTOR
INCIDENT
INFER
ISOLATED
PERSPECTIVE
PRIORITY
QUALIFY
RATIONALE
REASONABLE
RESTRICT
TYPICAL

Activity 2 Puzzle

ACROSS

1. All apartments here _____ of five rooms.
2. Anna wants to _____ children from the guest list.
5. _____ to the mayor, the new park will open next month.
6. I did not _____ any problems with the new machine.
11. It is _____ to expect courtesy from salespeople.
14. What was the _____ for canceling the concert?
15. Witches _____ in fairy tales.
17. When will I _____ for medical benefits?
18. Who reported the _____ to the police?
19. Pam needs to _____ her use of salt.

DOWN

1. What _____ are the judges using?
3. Childcare is _____ for single parents who work.
4. What is the top _____ for today?
7. When did the owner _____ the team needed a new coach?
8. Traffic was a _____ in our late arrival.
9. A picnic is a _____ summer activity.
10. The article was written from a nurse's _____.
12. Weather will often _____ people's moods.
13. Sam finds _____ places on the lake to fish.
16. Did you _____ from Shauna's tone of voice that she was angry?

Activity 3 Rewrite the Sentences

Rewrite these sentences using the correct forms of the vocabulary words from this unit to replace the underlined words. Underline all the vocabulary words you use.

Example: *The research says that* an active social life is a *very important* *thing that results* in living a long and healthy life.
<u>According</u> to the research, an active social life is a <u>crucial</u> <u>factor</u> in living a long and healthy life.

1. Because the area *is made up* of mountains and land that is *not near any towns*, you will not *meet or see* many people.

   _____

   _____

2. From the *view point* of a *common, average* teenager, parents *live* to *control and limit* their children.

   _____

   _____

3. Mika did not fill out an application, so I *had reason to probably think* that she did not *meet the requirements* for the job.

   _____

   _____

Activity 4 Use the Vocabulary Words

Complete the paragraph using the correct forms of the vocabulary words from this unit.

Civil Disobedience

Sometimes people _____ that a law is unjust and _____
                          1.   **2.**
people unfairly. They may believe a law _____ the rights of some
                                            3.
people or _____ a certain group of people. These reasons provide the
              4.
_____ for protest. Civil disobedience is a peaceful way to protest. Protesters
      5.
create _____ when they refuse to obey laws. The _____
          6.   **7.**
is nonviolence, so when protesters _____ violence, they respond peacefully.
                                        8.
This was a major _____ in the success of the civil rights movement.
                      9.

Unit 2

evolve

evident

imply

approach

trace

despite

valid

characteristic

data

hypothesis

role

origin

theory

distinguish

explicit

incompatible

specify

successive

clarify

eliminate

characteristic data approach evolve
distinguish specify despite **clarify** explicit
evident origin evolve hypothesis eliminate
incompatible role **imply** successive specify
distinguish trace data valid role **theory**

Vocabulary Knowledge Rating Chart

How well do you know the words? Use the numbers to rate your knowledge of the vocabulary words. Follow the teacher's directions.

4 = I know the word. I know it well enough to teach it to someone else.
3 = The word is familiar. I think I know what it means.
2 = I have heard the word, but I'm not sure what it means.
1 = I don't know the word at all.

	My rating before instruction	I think the word means	My rating after instruction
characteristic			
clarify			
evident			
imply			
theory			

Word Meaning Chart

Complete the chart. Follow the teacher's directions.

characteristic *(noun)* /kar ik tuh RIS tik/

A **characteristic** is a special feature that helps to identify a person or a thing.

EXAMPLES

One _____ of a fairy tale is animals that can speak.

Class Example: _____

My Example: One **characteristic** of a good student is _____

clarify *(verb)* /KLAR uh fahy/

To **clarify** is to make something easier to understand with further explanation or more details.

EXAMPLES

A teacher usually _____ instructions for students before they take a test.

Class Example: _____

My Example: One way to **clarify** directions to the airport is _____

evident *(adjective)* /EV i duhnt/

Evident means obvious, easily noticed.

EXAMPLES

The wind and dark clouds made it _____ that a storm was coming.

Class Example: _____

My Example: From the child's laughter, it was **evident** _____

imply *(verb)* /im PLAHY/

To **imply** is to suggest something without directly saying or showing it.

EXAMPLES

Amy did not say anything, but her facial expression _____ that she was upset.

Class Example: _____

My Example: During the class, the student's attitude **implied** _____

theory *(noun)* /THEER ee/   A **theory** is an idea of how or why something happens or works.

EXAMPLES

Scientists have more than one _____ about how dinosaurs disappeared.

Class Example: _____

My Example: Based on the evidence, the police had a **theory** that _____

Exercise 1 Use the Words

Complete each sentence. Write the correct form of the vocabulary word in the blank space.

1. The salesperson in the department store _____ that the toaster oven would be on sale next week.

2. At the news conference, the reporters asked the governor to _____ her position on unemployment.

3. Is there any truth to the _____ that dreams can help us understand ourselves?

4. Gordon's passion for teaching was _____ in the way he interacted with the children.

5. In the Minh family, a physical _____ that all the children share is brown eyes.

Exercise 2 Complete the Sentences

These sentences have been started for you. They are not complete. Complete them with your own words.

1. Lavette's body language implied _____

   _____

2. A characteristic I admire in a leader is _____

   _____

   _____

3. My theory about the popularity of computer games is _____

   _____

   _____

4. After the first day of school, it was evident to me that _____

   _____

   _____

5. I asked the doctor to clarify _____

   _____

   _____

Exercise 3 Words at Work

Circle the best answer to each multiple choice question below. Then write a brief response to the question that follows. Write your answers in complete sentences.

1. William is about to start a project at work that consists of several phases. Before he starts the project, he asks his manager to clarify the production schedule. Why does he do that?

   (A) The schedule is complex.   **(B)** The schedule is simple.   **(C)** There is no schedule.

   What is another reason to ask someone to clarify something? _____

   _____

   _____

2. Jonelle's manager is very pleased that he hired her. Since Jonelle has been working at the company, it is evident to her manager that she possesses several characteristics of an outstanding employee. What is one characteristic Jonelle possesses?

   (A) She wears fashionable   **(B)** She is cooperative with   **(C)** She brings her own lunch.
   clothes.   other employees.

   What is another characteristic Jonelle is likely to possess? _____

   _____

   _____

3. Eugenia folded the restaurant's tablecloths. Later, she noticed that Riga had refolded the tablecloths. What could Riga's actions imply?

   (A) The tablecloths were   **(B)** Riga likes to fold   **(C)** Eugenia had not folded
   folded properly.   tablecloths.   them properly.

   When have someone's actions implied that you did something wrong? _____

   _____

   _____

4. Tonight Alex informed his family, "I have a theory about how the dog got out of the yard this morning." What did he mean?

   (A) He knows for certain   **(B)** He has a picture to show   **(C)** He has an idea of what
   what happened.   what happened.   happened.

   When are people asked to provide a theory about something that happened? _____

   _____

   _____

Word Families

Most words are part of a family of words. Study the word families on this page. Then fill in the missing words using the correct form of each word.

---

characteristic *(noun)*

- characteristic *(adjective)*
  A Japanese beetle is identified by its characteristic metallic green body.

- characteristically *(adverb)*
  Dogs characteristically bark when they see a cat.

imply *(verb)*

- implication *(noun)*
  The implication of the poll is that voters have lost confidence in their governor.

clarify *(verb)*

- clarification *(noun)*
  The jury said it was unsure about the law and asked for clarification.

evident *(adjective)*

- evidently *(adverb)*
  The man was evidently tired because he kept yawning.

theory *(noun)*

- theorized *(adjective)*
  Isaac Newton theorized that the force of gravity pulls objects to the ground.

---

1. Rashid was unsure how to set up the printer, so he asked for _____.

2. Naomi's emails are _____ brief.

3. Ed _____ that employees who choose their hours are more productive.

4. Is a competitive spirit _____ of a winning team?

5. Soraya _____ enjoyed the play because she saw it twice.

Complete the paragraph using the correct forms of the five vocabulary words in this lesson. Each form of a word is used only once.

Popularity of Abraham Lincoln

Abraham Lincoln was not popular during his presidency. He only received 39 percent of

the popular vote in the 1860 election. It was _____ that many people
                                                        6.

disliked him. They laughed at his physical _____. He was not considered
                                                        7.

handsome. Their criticisms _____ that he was not intelligent. Lincoln
                                        8.

_____ responded to his opponents with humor, not criticism. Many
       9.

historians _____ that his strength of character made him an effective leader.
              10.

Many situations require a positive attitude.

Exercise 5 ## What Do You Think?

Read each question and write a brief answer. Explain your answers in complete sentences.

1. When do a person's positive characteristics need to be most evident—on a first date or a job interview?

   _____

   _____

   _____

2. If someone is characteristically late to work, does that imply that the person is not a dedicated worker?

   _____

   _____

   _____

3. Do parents always need to clarify their expectations of their children, or should children be able to infer what is expected of them?

   _____

   _____

Read the following passage. Answer the questions using complete sentences.

The Electoral College

The Electoral College is not a place to go to school. This "college" is a group of 538 people called electors. The electors have a crucial job to do—they vote to elect the president and vice-president of the United States.

The electors are from all 50 states and the District of Columbia. The number of electors for each state equals the number of a state's members in the House of Representatives and the Senate. Michigan, for example, has 17 electors because it has 15 House members and two senators. California has 55 electors because it has 53 House members and two senators.

People often are surprised to learn that the Electoral College exists. Most people think the voters elect the president. The voters do elect the president, but not directly. When people vote for a presidential candidate, they are actually telling the electors how they want the electors to vote.

Several weeks after a presidential election, the Electoral College meets to vote. Each elector has one vote. Electors cast their votes according to the results of the election in their state. For example, if the Republican candidate wins the election in Delaware, the Delaware electors vote for the Republican. The presidential candidate who receives 270 electoral votes or more wins the election.

When the country's Founding Fathers created the Electoral College system, their rationale included several factors. Their priority was to make sure the president was elected fairly. They were concerned that people would only vote for a person from their state or region. Consequently, they looked for a way to balance the power between the small states and big states. They also considered similar systems used throughout history.

They concluded that the Electoral College system was the most reasonable solution.

1. The Electoral College was based on the theory that the system would make voting fair among all the states. How does the Electoral College do this?

_____

_____

2. If you were asked to clarify why there are 538 electors in the Electoral College, how would you respond?

_____

_____

3. The Electoral College shares some characteristics with a similar system used in ancient Rome. What does that imply about the founders of the U.S.?

_____

_____

characteristic data approach evolve
distinguish specify despite **clarify** explicit
evident origin evolve hypothesis eliminate
incompatible role **imply** successive specify
distinguish trace data valid role **theory**

New Word List

☐ characteristic

☐ clarify

☐ evident

☐ imply

☐ theory

Review Word List

☐ _____

☐ _____

☐ _____

☐ _____

☐ _____

Exercise 7 Writing Connection

Write a brief response to each question. Use words from this lesson or previous lessons in your answer. Write your answers in complete sentences.

Think about the most evident characteristics of courtesy. Do you have a theory about why some people are more courteous than other people? Give a specific example.

_____

_____

_____

_____

_____

Think of a time when you were asked to clarify something (an opinion or explanation, for example). What was the situation? How was the clarification helpful? Be specific.

_____

_____

_____

_____

Exercise 8 Reflection

Think about the words you have studied in this lesson.

1. Which words did you enjoy learning? _____

2. Select one word and imagine where you will use the word. Explain the situation.

_____

_____

3. Which words do you still need help with? _____

4. Return to the Knowledge Rating Chart at the beginning of this lesson. Complete column 3. How have your responses changed?

characteristic **data** approach imply distinguish
evolve specify clarify despite explicit
origin evident **hypothesis** eliminate
incompatible role successive imply **specify**
approach **valid** trace distinguish theory role

Vocabulary Knowledge Rating Chart

How well do you know the words? Use the numbers to rate your knowledge of the vocabulary words. Follow the teacher's directions.

4 = I know the word. I know it well enough to teach it to someone else.
3 = The word is familiar. I think I know what it means.
2 = I have heard the word, but I'm not sure what it means.
1 = I don't know the word at all.

	My rating before instruction	I think the word means	My rating after instruction
data			
evolve			
hypothesis			
specify			
valid			

Word Meaning Chart

Complete the chart. Follow the teacher's directions.

data *(noun)* /DEY tuh/

Data is a set of facts, statistics, and other information used for study or analysis.

EXAMPLES

The scientist collected and analyzed the _____ before publishing the report.

Class Example: _____

My Example: Personal **data** that I am careful about giving out includes _____

evolve *(verb)* /ih VOLV/

To **evolve** means to develop or change gradually over time.

EXAMPLES

Blue jeans _____ from work clothes to designer clothing.

Class Example: _____

My Example: An electronic item that has **evolved** in the last five years is _____

hypothesis *(noun)* /hahy POTH uh sis/

A **hypothesis** is an explanation based on evidence that has not been tested or proven to be true.

EXAMPLES

The _____ of global warming has not yet been proven.

Class Example: _____

My Example: More research is needed to prove the **hypothesis** that using cell phones _____

_____

specify *(verb)* /SPES uh fahy/

To **specify** is to state or identify something exactly, clearly, or definitely.

EXAMPLES

The salesperson asked us to _____ the color and fabric design we wanted for the sofa.

Class Example: _____

My Example: The doctor did not **specify** _____

valid *(adjective)* /VAL id/

Valid tells that something is legal, official, or based on truth or logic.

EXAMPLES

A _____ password often consists of a combination of letters and numbers.

Class Example: _____

My Example: Lana gave a **valid** excuse for being late when she said, "_____"

Exercise 1 Use the Words

Complete each sentence. Write the correct form of the vocabulary word in the blank space.

1. George was unable to travel internationally because he did not have a

   _____ passport.

2. The article supported the _____ that the stress of losing a job can cause high blood pressure.

3. Scientists measure the size of stars by using the _____ collected from space satellites.

4. A childhood nickname often _____ from a unique physical or behavioral characteristic of a child.

5. Did Ms. Chung _____ the factors affecting her decision to change jobs?

Exercise 2 Complete the Sentences

These sentences have been started for you. They are not complete. Complete them with your own words.

1. A valid concern that parents have is _____

   _____

2. Trust is a feeling that needs to evolve because _____

   _____

   _____

3. I would like to have more data about _____ because _____

   _____

   _____

4. The rules at our school clearly specify that _____

   _____

   _____

5. A hypothesis I have about children who watch too much television is _____

   _____

   _____

Words at Work

Circle the best answer to each multiple choice question below. Then write a brief response to the question that follows. Write your answers in complete sentences.

1. Pedro works as a parking valet for a large restaurant. The uniform requirements specify dark pants, a white shirt, and a red tie. They also specify that any shoes, except sandals, may be worn. What is Pedro wearing this evening?

   (A) a white jacket and a red tie   **(B)** a dark shirt and a red tie   **(C)** a pair of dark athletic shoes

   When have you been in a situation that specified the kind of clothing you needed to wear?

   _____

   _____

2. At ADZ Paper Factory, there were so many schedule problems that the owners created a new regulation. It stated that employees needed a valid reason to request a schedule change. Which of the following reasons qualifies as valid?

   (A) a specially televised soccer game   **(B)** a child's performance in a school concert   **(C)** a one-day special sale

   What is another valid reason to request a schedule change? _____

   _____

3. Marla recently received a certificate for being with the company for 15 years. Marla's supervisor said, "I remember when you started working here. You have evolved into a confident and competent employee." What words best describe Marla when she began working?

   (A) insecure and shy   **(B)** secure and outgoing   **(C)** skilled and efficient

   How do you think Marla evolved into a confident and competent employee? _____

   _____

4. The managers of Shining Star Restaurant met to discuss the decrease in lunch sales. Leon, the newest manager, presented his hypothesis that the menu was boring and should be updated. "More customers will come in if there are newer items on the menu," he said. How can the restaurant test Leon's hypothesis?

   (A) create new sandwich specials   **(B)** print more colorful menus   **(C)** expand the lunch hours

   What is another possible hypothesis to explain the decrease in lunch sales? _____

   _____

Exercise 4 Word Families

Most words are part of a family of words. Study the word families on this page. Then fill in the missing words using the correct form of each word.

---

evolve *(verb)*

- evolution *(noun)*
  Black musicians were mainly responsible for the evolution of jazz.

specify *(verb)*

- specified *(adjective)*
  Use only the exact ingredients in the specified amounts if you want a perfect pie.

hypothesis *(noun)*

- hypothesize *(verb)*
  The senators hypothesized that more regulations would make cars safer.

valid *(adjective)*

- validity *(noun)*
  The reporter questioned the validity of the census data.
- validate *(verb)*
  The witness validated Henry's statement that the truck went through the red light.

---

1. Not following test directions accurately will affect the _____ of the test results.

2. Use the coupon before the _____ date if you want the discount.

3. Why did the firefighters _____ that the fire was caused by a camper?

4. The test results _____ Dr. Garza's diagnosis.

5. The _____ of the use of Arabic numbers in Europe took a long time.

Complete the paragraph using the correct forms of the five vocabulary words in this lesson. Each form of a word is used only once.

Space Technology

For many years, scientists relied on telescopes to study the planets. As technology has

_____, so has the ability to collect _____.
          6.   **7.**

Scientists use satellite images to land spacecraft in _____ locations on
                                                            8.

planets, such as Mars. The _____ of unmanned spacecraft has allowed
                               9.

scientists to explore isolated and unknown areas. As a result, scientists have been able to test

the _____ of many _____ and create new theories.
         10.   **11.**

It is _____ to _____ that space exploration will
          12.   **13.**

continue for years to come.

The use of cash, bank cards, and credit cards has evolved over the years.

Exercise 5 What Do You Think?

Read each question and write a brief answer. Explain your answers in complete sentences.

1. Is it valid to hypothesize that cash will cease to exist in the future and everyone will use bank or credit cards instead?

_____

_____

_____

2. For whose job is it more crucial to validate data—a police officer or a scientist?

_____

_____

_____

3. Is it valid to assume that all personal relationships evolve over time?

_____

_____

_____

Reading Connection

Read the following passage. Answer the questions using complete sentences.

Clarence Birdseye—The Father of Frozen Food

The next time you buy a frozen pizza or package of vegetables, think of Clarence Birdseye. In the 1920s, he invented a way to quick-freeze food so it remained fresh and flavorful.

Clarence Birdseye had a spirit of adventure as a young man and did not finish college. Instead he went to Labrador in northeast Canada in 1912 to trap animals for the fur trade. When he returned to the United States, he got married and had a child.

Birdseye took his family back to Labrador in 1916 to work as a researcher. Part of his job was to study the native people of Labrador. Daily life for the Birdseye family was difficult. Their diet was restricted to mostly fish and some meat, such as reindeer or caribou. Vegetables were very rare and only available when a ship brought them in.

In this isolated northern part of the world, winter temperatures get very cold. Birdseye began experimenting with the method of quick-freezing food used by the native people. He filled a barrel of cabbages with salt water. In the extreme cold, the water and cabbages froze quickly. Birdseye chopped through the ice to get a cabbage for the family's dinner. When it thawed, the cabbage tasted fresh.

Birdseye also experimented with quick-freezing fish and caribou meat. The results were the same. The food tasted fresh. Freezing food was nothing new, but Birdseye concluded that the quick-freezing method was crucial to preserving freshness and flavor.

Birdseye kept notes on all his experiments. When the family returned to the United States, he invented a way to quick-freeze foods. He started Birdseye Seafoods in 1923 to sell frozen fish. He sold the company in 1929 for $22 million. His name lives on in the Birds Eye brand of frozen foods.

1. What was the hypothesis that Clarence Birdseye tested with his experiments in Labrador?

_____

_____

2. What data did Birdseye use to show that his hypothesis was valid?

_____

_____

3. How has the evolution of frozen foods affected the typical American lifestyle?

_____

_____

characteristic **data** approach imply distinguish
evolve specify clarity despite explicit
origin evident **hypothesis** eliminate
incompatible role successive imply **specify**
approach **valid** trace distinguish theory role

New Word List

☐ data

☐ evolve

☐ hypothesis

☐ specify

☐ valid

Review Word List

☐ _____

☐ _____

☐ _____

☐ _____

☐ _____

Writing Connection

Write a brief response to each question. Use words from this lesson or previous lessons in your answer. Write your answers in complete sentences.

In what ways have you seen a family member or friend evolve? What factors contributed to this evolution? Specify the changes you have observed.

_____

_____

_____

_____

_____

There are times when it is necessary to specify directions, needs, or other information. When have you had to specify information? Describe the situation. Explain why it was necessary for you to be specific. What could have happened if you were not specific?

_____

_____

_____

_____

_____

_____

Reflection

Think about the words you have studied in this lesson.

1. Which words did you enjoy learning? _____

2. Select one word and imagine where you will use the word. Explain the situation.

_____

_____

3. Which words do you still need help with? _____

4. Return to the Knowledge Rating Chart at the beginning of this lesson. Complete column 3. How have your responses changed?

characteristic data **approach** distinguish

evolve **despite** role specify clarify explicit

hypothesis evident origin **eliminate**

incompatible successive imply specify

distinguish trace data **role** theory valid

Vocabulary Knowledge Rating Chart

How well do you know the words? Use the numbers to rate your knowledge of the vocabulary words. Follow the teacher's directions.

4 = I know the word. I know it well enough to teach it to someone else.
3 = The word is familiar. I think I know what it means.
2 = I have heard the word, but I'm not sure what it means.
1 = I don't know the word at all.

	My rating before instruction	I think the word means	My rating after instruction
approach			
despite			
eliminate			
incompatible			
role			

Word Meaning Chart

Complete the chart. Follow the teacher's directions.

approach *(verb)* /uh PROHCH/

To **approach** means to move closer in distance, time, or criteria.

EXAMPLES

When the mail carrier _____ the house, the dog began to bark.

Class Example: _____

My Example: As summer vacation **approaches**, students feel _____

despite *(preposition)* /dih SPAHYT/

Despite means that one thing does not affect or change another thing.

EXAMPLES

Bertha was hired for the job _____ the fact that she did not have any experience.

Class Example: _____

My Example: **Despite** the rain, _____

eliminate *(verb)* /ih LIM uh neyt/

To **eliminate** means to remove, exclude, or get rid of something.

EXAMPLES

On a timed, multiple-choice test, students should _____ incorrect answers quickly.

Class Example: _____

My Example: To lose weight, I recommend you **eliminate** _____ from your diet.

incompatible *(adjective)* /in kuhm PAT uh buhl/

Incompatible means that people or things cannot exist together because they are too different.

EXAMPLES

Bleach and ammonia are _____ household products because they are dangerous when mixed.

Class Example: _____

My Example: Eating _____ is **incompatible** with being a vegetarian.

role *(noun)* /rohl/

A **role** is the way someone or something is involved in a situation.

EXAMPLES

Thomas Jefferson had a key _____ in writing the Declaration of Independence.

Class Example: _____

My Example: Computers play a _____ **role** in my typical day because _____

Use the Words

Complete each sentence. Write the correct form of the vocabulary word in the blank space.

1. Helen Keller was a well-known speaker and writer _____ being deaf and blind.

2. Did the label specify that the software was _____ with older versions of the operating system?

3. The purpose of the semifinal round of the tournament is to _____ two of the four teams.

4. Your _____ as the host consists of making the guests feel comfortable and welcome.

5. As the president _____ the halfway mark in his term, the polls showed support for his economic policy.

Complete the Sentences

These sentences have been started for you. They are not complete. Complete them with your own words.

1. The company eliminated more than 50 jobs because _____

   _____

   _____

2. Parents can take an active role in their children's education by _____

   _____

   _____

3. Something that is incompatible with a democratic society is _____

   _____

   _____

4. Despite the terrible traffic, _____

   _____

   _____

5. When a police officer approaches me, I feel _____ because _____

   _____

Words at Work

Circle the best answer to each multiple choice question below. Then write a brief response to the question that follows. Write your answers in complete sentences.

1. Curtis told his manager, "I'm ready for more responsibilities and a bigger role in our work unit." What would Curtis like?

   (A) a schedule change   **(B)** a job promotion   **(C)** a job reference

   What can you infer about Curtis from his desire to have a bigger role at work? _____

   _____

   _____

2. Debra has a long commute to work and an inconvenient schedule. Despite these factors, she decided not to look for a job closer to home. What do you suppose was part of her rationale for keeping her job?

   (A) partial medical benefits   **(B)** an attractive uniform   **(C)** a long lunch break

   What is another factor for someone to decide to stay in a job despite inconvenient

   working conditions? _____

   _____

   _____

3. At a bank managers' meeting, Ms. Felton said, "From my perspective, one of our trainees, Edgar, is quickly approaching the level of competence necessary to work on his own." What did Ms. Felton mean?

   (A) Edgar is ready to work   **(B)** Edgar will be ready to   **(C)** Edgar needs a lot more
          alone now.   work alone very soon.   time before working alone.

   How do you know when you are approaching a level of competence in something? _____

   _____

   _____

4. Danna and Liz constantly complain to their manager about each other. Danna is talkative and likes loud music. Liz is quiet and prefers to work without noise. Their manager, Mr. Bell, decided they were incompatible. What did he do?

   (A) changed their   **(B)** changed their   **(C)** changed their
          break times   work badges   work shifts

   How do incompatible employees affect their coworkers? _____

   _____

Exercise 4 Word Families

Most words are part of a family of words. Study the word families on this page. Then fill in the missing words using the correct form of each word.

---

approach *(verb)*
- approach *(noun)*
  The passengers fastened their seat belts as the plane began its approach to the runway.

eliminate *(verb)*
- elimination *(noun)*
  The elimination of slavery was the goal of the abolitionist movement prior to the Civil War.

incompatible *(adjective)*
- incompatibility *(noun)*
  The incompatibility of their blood types was the reason the spouses could not donate blood to each other.

role *(noun)*
- role model *(noun)*
  Positive role models, like professional athletes, provide children with examples of success and achievement.

---

1. I found a phone charger. However, it is _____ with my phone.

2. Credit and bank cards have _____ the need to carry much cash.

3. "It is evident," Dr. Wu concluded, "that the _____ of the winter holidays can cause some people stress."

4. The _____ of lead in children's toys has saved many lives.

5. The company did not get a permit for its building because of the _____ of the design with other city buildings.

Complete the paragraph using the correct forms of the five vocabulary words in this lesson. Each form of a word is used only once.

Polio

In the early 1950s, the _____ of summer frightened parents. Parents
6.

worried about polio, a highly infectious disease that could paralyze children. Swimming in pools,

for example, could infect their children. _____ parents' best efforts,
7.

children could easily get the polio virus. Normal summer fun was _____
8.

with the need to restrict children's activities. Two scientists had key _____
9.

in helping to _____ this terrible disease. Dr. Jonas Salk developed the first
10.

polio vaccine. Later, Dr. Albert Sabin created an oral vaccine. These vaccines were responsible

for the _____ of the disease and the public's great fear of it.
11.

Despite their convenience, plastic bags contribute to environmental problems.

Exercise 5 What Do You Think?

Read each question and write a brief answer. Explain your answers in complete sentences.

1. Is it possible for stores to eliminate all plastic bags despite their popularity?

_____

_____

_____

2. Obesity is a major health problem today. Who should take an active role in helping children eliminate bad eating habits—schools or parents?

_____

_____

_____

3. Is it possible for an incompatible couple to eliminate their differences?

_____

_____

_____

Reading Connection

Read the following passage. Answer the questions using complete sentences.

What Is Classical Music?

Three hundred years ago in Europe, there was no hip-hop, rock, country, or jazz music. There were no superstars. Huge stadiums that could hold thousands of music fans at a concert did not exist.

Music, however, was very important to Europeans. In cities like Vienna and Paris, people went to concert halls to listen to classical music. The "stars" of the day were the composers who wrote the music. Johann Sebastian Bach, Franz Hayden, Wolfgang Mozart, and Ludwig von Beethoven wrote music that is still popular today. You can hear it played on the radio and at concerts with an orchestra. In addition, classical music is used in movies and television commercials.

What are some of the differences between classical and modern music? Classical music is written for instruments like the piano and violin. In a lot of modern music, the guitar is the important instrument.

Jazz musicians often improvise, or make up, what they are playing. Classical composers, however, carefully write down what they want each instrument to play and at what tempo, or speed. A typical rock song may last for three or four minutes, while a piece of classical music lasts much longer. A symphony, for example, consists of four different sections and can be thirty minutes long.

Hip-hop and salsa make people want to dance and sing along. Classical music is more formal. People sit quietly and listen to an orchestra play the music. Through the music, listeners imagine a story, a scene, or feel an emotion. Antonio Vivaldi's *The Four Seasons*, for example, inspires a person's imagination. Through the instruments, Vivaldi created musical pictures of the characteristics of the different seasons: singing birds and buzzing mosquitoes, a summer rainstorm, children ice-skating, and warm winter fires.

1. What type of audience behavior is incompatible with a classical music concert?

   _____

   _____

2. As we approach the 225th anniversary of Mozart's death, his music is still universally popular. What does that imply about the kind of music he composed?

   _____

   _____

3. What is the role of music in people's lives? Do classical and modern music have the same role or different roles?

   _____

   _____

characteristic data **approach** distinguish
evolve **despite** role specify clarify explicit
hypothesis evident origin **eliminate**
incompatible successive imply specify
distinguish trace data **role** theory valid

New Word List

☐ approach

☐ despite

☐ eliminate

☐ incompatible

☐ role

Review Word List

☐ _____

☐ _____

☐ _____

☐ _____

☐ _____

Exercise 7 Writing Connection

Write a brief response to each question. Use words from this lesson or previous lessons in your answer. Write your answers in complete sentences.

What kind of a person would be incompatible with you? Describe the characteristics and behaviors that would make you and this person incompatible.

_____

_____

_____

_____

_____

What is a habit you have now that you would like to eliminate? Why? How did this habit evolve?

_____

_____

_____

_____

_____

Exercise 8 Reflection

Think about the words you have studied in this lesson.

1. Which words did you enjoy learning? _____

2. Select one word and imagine where you will use the word. Explain the situation.

   _____

   _____

3. Which words do you still need help with? _____

4. Return to the Knowledge Rating Chart at the beginning of this lesson. Complete column 3. How have your responses changed?

characteristic data approach **distinguish**

evolve **explicit** specify clarify despite

evident hypothesis **origin** data eliminate

successive incompatible role specify

distinguish data theory valid **trace** imply

Vocabulary Knowledge Rating Chart

How well do you know the words? Use the numbers to rate your knowledge of the vocabulary words. Follow the teacher's directions.

4 = I know the word. I know it well enough to teach it to someone else.
3 = The word is familiar. I think I know what it means.
2 = I have heard the word, but I'm not sure what it means.
1 = I don't know the word at all.

	My rating before instruction	I think the word means	My rating after instruction
distinguish			
explicit			
origin			
successive			
trace			

Word Meaning Chart

Complete the chart. Follow the teacher's directions.

distinguish (verb) /dih STING gwish/

To **distinguish** is to make someone or something different or to recognize the difference between people or things.

EXAMPLES

An African elephant's larger size _____ it from the smaller Asian elephant.

Class Example: _____

My Example: Something that **distinguishes** me from other members of my family is _____

explicit (adjective) /ik SPLIS it/

Explicit tells that something is expressed in a clear, direct way.

EXAMPLES

The instructions on the application are _____: use blue or black ink only.

Class Example: _____

My Example: Larry's doctor gave him **explicit** advice to _____

origin (noun) /OR i jin/

Origin means where or when something started.

EXAMPLES

Words like *psychologist* and *pharmacy* have a Greek _____ .

Class Example: _____

My Example: My family's **origins** are _____

successive (adjective) /suhk SES iv/

Successive means one after another.

EXAMPLES

Five _____ days of heavy rain caused severe flash flooding.

Class Example: _____

My Example: I have worked as a _____ for _____ **successive** _____

trace (verb) /treys/

To **trace** is to follow, study, or determine the history or beginning of something.

EXAMPLES

Historians can _____ the origin of soccer to China nearly 3,000 years ago.

Class Example: _____

My Example: Firefighters **traced** the start of the apartment fire to _____

Exercise 1 Use the Words

Complete each sentence. Write the correct form of the vocabulary word in the blank space.

1. Halloween has its _____ in ancient harvest celebrations.

2. The historical map on page 38 _____ the pioneers' journey across the Rocky Mountains.

3. Can a baby _____ her mother's voice from another woman's voice?

4. Although the patient is quite ill, his doctors expect him to improve with each

   _____ treatment.

5. In an e-mail to her mother, Georgina gave an _____ description of her wedding gown.

Exercise 2 Complete the Sentences

These sentences have been started for you. They are not complete. Complete them with your own words.

1. Something that required me to make successive attempts was _____

   _____

   _____

2. Young children are not always able to distinguish _____

   _____

   _____

3. One thing I know about the origin of the United States is that _____

   _____

   _____

4. To trace my family's history, I would start by _____

   _____

   _____

5. At school or work, I try to be explicit when _____

   _____

   _____

Words at Work

Circle the best answer to each multiple choice question below. Then write a brief response to the question that follows. Write your answers in complete sentences.

1. Ahmed was born in Libya but lives in England. He is applying to study in Canada. On the application, he must indicate his country of origin. What will he write in the space provided?

   (A) England   **(B)** Canada   **(C)** Libya

   What do you write when an application asks for your country of origin? _____

   _____

   _____

2. Mary-Rose works in the billing department of a plumbing company. Her major responsibility is to trace billing mistakes. How does she do that?

   (A) She refers to a customer's   **(B)** She approaches a   **(C)** She distinguishes a
      billing data.   customer's billing data.   customer's billing data.

   What specific information may help to trace a billing mistake? _____

   _____

   _____

3. Nancy and Greta are identical twins. They are servers at the Wagon Wheel Restaurant. Despite the fact that they have different hair styles, customers are often not able to distinguish Nancy from Greta. The restaurant manager, however, is always able to distinguish one from another. How is that possible?

   (A) Greta has green eyes and   **(B)** Nancy has a small scar   **(C)** They wear the same uniform.
      so does Nancy.   on her left cheek.

   What can Nancy and Greta do to help others distinguish them from one another? _____

   _____

4. The company's policy on absences is explicit. The employee handbook specifies that employees must provide a doctor's note if they are absent for three or more successive days. Rodney was ill this week and was absent on Monday, Tuesday, and Friday. Does he need to provide a doctor's note?

   (A) Yes, he was absent for   **(B)** No, he was absent for   **(C)** Yes, the company policy
      three successive days.   two successive days.   is explicit.

   What other explicit information is in an employee handbook? _____

   _____

Word Families

Most words are part of a family of words. Study the word families on this page. Then fill in the missing words using the correct form of each word.

---

distinguish *(verb)*

- distinguishing *(adjective)*
  A scar is a distinguishing feature.

origin *(noun)*

- originate *(verb)*
  The Olympics originated in ancient Greece.

- original *(adjective)*
  Pennsylvania was one of the original thirteen colonies.

- originally *(adverb)*
  Lisa is originally from Wisconsin, but she now lives in Texas.

explicit *(adjective)*

- explicitly *(adverb)*
  The police captain's report explicitly connected the presence of graffiti to crime.

successive *(adjective)*

- successively *(adverb)*
  As winter approaches, the days become successively shorter.

---

1. Hurricanes that affect the United States _____ in the Atlantic Ocean.

2. The witness _____ described the car accident to the police.

3. The temperature became _____ hotter during the week-long heat wave.

4. Much of the Bible was _____ written in Greek and Hebrew.

5. What is a _____ architectural feature of the new stadium?

Complete the paragraph using the correct forms of the five vocabulary words in this lesson. Each form of a word is used only once.

Interstate 95

Interstate 95, or I-95, is often called the Main Street of the East Coast of the United States.

I-95 _____ in Florida and ends near the Canadian border in Maine. It is
      6.

1,925 miles long. Its length _____ it as the country's longest north-south
                              7.

interstate highway. Construction of the _____ sections of the highway can
                                         8.

be _____ to 1957. Another _____ feature is I-95's
   9.   **10.**

importance to commerce and tourism. The use of I-95 has grown _____
                                                                11.

heavier over the years. Today, approximately 5 million cars travel on I-95 every day.

How do voters distinguish between candidates running for office?

What Do You Think?

Read each question and write a brief answer. Explain your answers in complete sentences.

1. What information best helps voters distinguish between different candidates—
explicit answers about issues or a short history of how they voted on past issues?

_____

_____

2. If successive generations of a family have lived in one place, is there a need for the
family to trace its origins?

_____

_____

_____

3. Can the origin of someone's success or failure usually be traced to one individual,
event, or moment in the person's life?

_____

_____

Reading Connection

Read the following passage. Answer the questions using complete sentences.

The Continents of the World

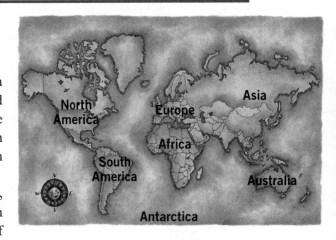

What is the difference between a country and a continent? A continent is one of seven very large land areas. Five of the seven continents contain most of the world's countries. Refer to the map to locate the seven continents as you read about them. They are listed in size, from largest to smallest.

Asia contains the highest point on earth, Mt. Everest, and the lowest point, the Dead Sea. Almost 4 billion people live in 49 Asian countries. More than 1 billion of them live in China. Another billion live in India.

Africa contains the world's largest desert, the Sahara, and the longest river, the Nile. Scientists theorize that humans originated in Africa. One billion people live in Africa.

North America consists of Canada, the United States, Mexico, Central America, the Caribbean islands, and Greenland, which is the largest island in the world. North America's population is about 529 million.

South America has the world's longest mountain range, the Andes, and the highest waterfall, Angel Falls in Venezuela. South America has a population of 386 million.

Antarctica, at the South Pole, is the windiest and most isolated place on the planet. It is also the coldest—the average temperature is -58°F. There are no trees or flowers. Penguins, seals, and other ocean creatures are found in Antarctica.

Europe is divided from Asia by the Ural Mountains in Russia. Today, 730 million people live in 45 European countries. Europe has had an important role in civilization for the last 600 years. Europeans colonized the Americas, Africa, Australia, and parts of Asia.

Australia is both a continent and a country. Besides rare animals like the kangaroo, 21 million people live in Australia.

1. What are two features that explicitly distinguish Asia from Europe?

   _____

   _____

2. On which continent do scientists believe they can trace the origin of human beings?

   _____

   _____

3. Is it valid to infer that conditions in Antarctica are incompatible with human survival needs? Provide explicit examples to explain your answer.

   _____

   _____

characteristic data approach **distinguish**
evolve **explicit** specify clarify despite
evident hypothesis **origin** data eliminate
successive incompatible role specify
distinguish data theory valid **trace** imply

New Word List

- ☐ distinguish
- ☐ explicit
- ☐ origin
- ☐ successive
- ☐ trace

Review Word List

- ☐ _____
- ☐ _____
- ☐ _____
- ☐ _____
- ☐ _____

Exercise 7 # Writing Connection

Write a brief response to each question. Use words from this lesson or previous lessons in your answer. Write your answers in complete sentences.

Think of a person you admire. What characteristic does that person possess that distinguishes him or her from other people you know? Is it the person's perspective or another quality that distinguishes him or her? Give explicit examples.

_____

_____

_____

_____

_____

Imagine you have applied for a new job. Your application has been accepted. The next step in the hiring process is a day of three successive interviews with different individuals in the company. How will you prepare yourself? What kinds of questions do you imagine you will encounter at the interviews?

_____

_____

_____

_____

Exercise 8 # Reflection

Think about the words you have studied in this lesson.

1. Which words did you enjoy learning? _____

2. Select one word and imagine where you will use the word. Explain the situation.

_____

_____

3. Which words do you still need help with? _____

4. Return to the Knowledge Rating Chart at the beginning of this lesson. Complete column 3. How have your responses changed?

Activity 1 ## Make Statements

Look at the picture of scientists working in a research laboratory. Then, write five statements about the picture. Use one or more of the vocabulary words you studied in this unit in each sentence. You may use words from the previous unit. <u>Underline</u> each vocabulary word you use.

Use this chart to choose different ways to make statements.

Make an observation:	Give an opinion:
There is/There are...	I think...
I notice that...	In my opinion/From my perspective...
It seems that...	It is important/It is essential...

Examples: Scientists use microscopes to identify <u>characteristics</u> that help <u>distinguish</u> one cell from another.
From my <u>perspective</u>, each <u>hypothesis</u> is important and should be tested.

_____

_____

_____

_____

_____

_____

_____

WORD BANK

APPROACH
CHARACTERISTIC
CLARIFY
DATA
DESPITE
DISTINGUISH
ELIMINATE
EVIDENT
EVOLVE
EXPLICIT
HYPOTHESIS
IMPLY
INCOMPATIBLE
ORIGIN
ROLE
SPECIFY
SUCCESSIVE
THEORY
TRACE
VALID

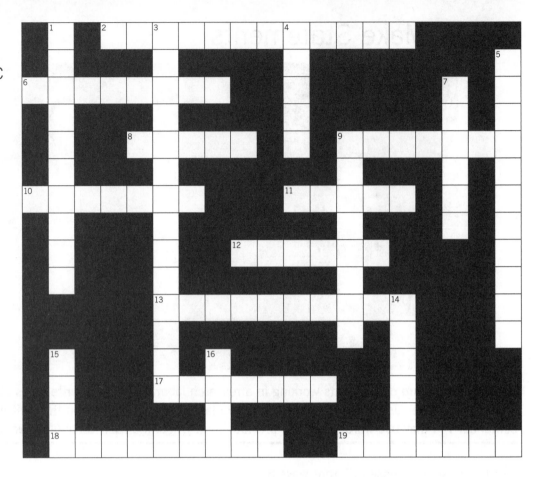

Activity 2 Puzzle

ACROSS

2. Why were you and your roommate _____?

6. Good servers _____ customers with a smile.

8. The card has expired so it is not _____.

9. It was _____ that no one was home.

10. _____ the weather, we had a great vacation.

11. Did Mr. Lan _____ you lost the keys?

12. The librarian can explain the _____ of our town.

13. After ten _____ days of work, Lou got a day off.

17. Can you _____ the meaning of this word for me?

18. Is it possible to _____ all sugar from a diet?

19. Please _____ the number of tickets you need.

DOWN

1. Do not believe a _____ until it has been proven.

3. Curiosity is a _____ of young children.

4. Was your mechanic able to _____ the cause of the problem?

5. An accent can _____ an American from a British speaker.

7. One _____ is that the robber worked alone.

9. Steve always gives clear and _____ directions.

14. How did our plans for a small dinner _____ into a large party?

15. Attitude plays an important _____ in a person's mental health.

16. You need to check the _____ before writing the report.

Activity 3 Rewrite the Sentences

Use the correct forms of the vocabulary words from this unit to replace the underlined words. Underline all the vocabulary words you use.

Example: Because of computer problems, attempts *one after another* were needed to *remove* all the personal *information* of former clients.
Because of computer problems, <u>successive</u> attempts were needed to <u>eliminate</u> all the personal <u>data</u> of former clients.

1. The announcer *clearly stated* that all ticket holders should *come near* the gate with a *legally acceptable* ID.

   _____

2. Did you have a *part* in *studying and determining the history of* the *beginnings* of your family name?

   _____

3. The counselor *indirectly suggested* that it was *obvious* to everyone that Erma and Phil were *too different to live or work together*.

   _____

Activity 4 Complete the Paragraph

Use the correct forms of the vocabulary words from this unit. Each word is used only once.

Louis Pasteur, Father of the Germ Theory

In his _____ as a chemist and biologist, Louis Pasteur did research.
1.
He collected _____ to prove the _____ that germs
2.   3.
cause disease. This was not _____ to people in the 1800s. The results of
4.
Pasteur's _____ experiments convinced people that the germ theory was
5.
_____. Pasteur gave hospitals _____ instructions to use
6.   7.
high heat on medical instruments to kill microbes, or germs. _____ initial
8.
doubt, the practice of sterilizing medical supplies began to _____. Doctors
9.
soon understood it was necessary to _____ germs to prevent infection. This
10.
was the _____ of the science of microbiology.
11.

Unit 3

anticipate

implication

generate

aspect

extent

pursue

diverse

impose

standard

ambiguous

maintain

dominate

subsequent

integral

illustrate

underlying

submit

context

substantial

furthermore

context furthermore anticipate ambiguous
impose submit **dominate** aspect extent
implication pursue generate diverse
integral illustrate **maintain** standard
underlying **substantial** subsequent submit

Vocabulary Knowledge Rating Chart

How well do you know the words? Use the numbers to rate your knowledge of the vocabulary words. Follow the teacher's directions.

4 = I know the word. I know it well enough to teach it to someone else.
3 = The word is familiar. I think I know what it means.
2 = I have heard the word, but I'm not sure what it means.
1 = I don't know the word at all.

	My rating before instruction	I think the word means	My rating after instruction
context			
dominate			
implication			
maintain			
substantial			

Word Meaning Chart

Complete the chart. Follow the teacher's directions.

---

context *(noun)* /KON tekst/

A **context** is the situation, circumstances, or information that provides a specific meaning and understanding of something.

EXAMPLES

The math teacher used a baseball _____ to explain the concept of percentages.

Class Example: _____

My Example: It helps to know the historical **context** when you read _____

---

dominate *(verb)* /DOM uh neyt/

To **dominate** means to have control or influence over someone or something.

EXAMPLES

Keisha _____ the conversation. No one else had a chance to speak.

Class Example: _____

My Example: _____ **dominated** the news for several days.

---

implication *(noun)* /im pli KEY shuhn/

An **implication** is a possible consequence or result.

EXAMPLES

Lengthening the school day could have significant _____ for working parents.

Class Example: _____

My Example: One **implication** of raising gas prices is _____

---

maintain *(verb)* /meyn TEYN/

To **maintain** means to keep something in the same state, condition, or level.

EXAMPLES

For some people it is a challenge to _____ their weight after dieting.

Class Example: _____

My Example: One way to **maintain** a car is _____

---

substantial *(adjective)* /suhb STAN shuhl/

Substantial means that something is large in size, degree, or importance.

EXAMPLES

Kendra bought a new oven because she received a _____ tax refund this year.

Class Example: _____

My Example: A **substantial** amount of effort is required to _____

Exercise 1 Use the Words

Complete each sentence. Write the correct form of the vocabulary word in the blank space.

1. Despite the recent clean-up, a _____ amount of trash remained on the bike path.

2. What are the financial _____ of the city's decision to expand the recycling facilities?

3. The independent candidate, Anne Claxton, _____ the debate with her clear, explicit responses.

4. The newspaper printed only a few lines of the speech, so the mayor's comments were taken out of _____.

5. It is crucial for senior citizens to _____ their independence as long as possible.

Exercise 2 Complete the Sentences

These sentences have been started for you. They are not complete. Complete them with your own words.

1. Our team began to dominate the game when _____

_____

_____

2. A good way to maintain a friendly relationship with a neighbor is _____

_____

_____

3. It is important to know the context of a person's actions or words because _____

_____

_____

4. I would offer a substantial reward if _____

_____

_____

5. There could be serious implications if _____

_____

_____

Exercise 3 Words at Work

Circle the best answer to each multiple choice question below. Then write a brief response to the question that follows. Write your answers in complete sentences.

1. Marco gave Mrs. Wilson an estimate to paint her kitchen and dining room. He told her it would take a substantial amount of time to remove the wallpaper in the kitchen before painting. What can you conclude from Marco's comment?

   (A) The job will take longer and cost less.

   (B) The job will take longer and cost more.

   (C) The job will take less time and cost more.

   What is another job that takes a substantial amount of time to perform? _____

   _____

2. Vicki works in the customer service department of a large department store. At her orientation, she was told that it is crucial to maintain a positive attitude despite a customer's inappropriate comments or rude behavior. How does Vicki maintain a good attitude?

   (A) She smiles when she speaks to customers.

   (B) She writes down customers' names.

   (C) She works behind the counter.

   How do you maintain a good attitude at school or work despite negative encounters with

   classmates, coworkers, or customers? _____

   _____

3. The owners of Liberty Cleaners announced to employees that they would be moving to a new location by the end of the year. The new location is not near a bus stop, but it does have substantial parking. What is one implication of this move for employees?

   (A) Many may have parking problems.

   (B) Several will not be able to drive to work.

   (C) Some may have difficulty getting to work.

   What is another implication of this move to a new location? _____

   _____

4. Starting next week, all employees at the Shutters South factory, including the managers, are required to wear a photo ID at work. Many employees initially complained until they learned the context in which the decision was made. What detail was part of the context?

   (A) two incidents of unknown people walking through the factory

   (B) two employees are photographers who can take employees' pictures

   (C) many factories require employees to wear badges

   How do you think knowing the context made the employees feel? Why? _____

   _____

Exercise 4 Word Families

Most words are part of a family of words. Study the word families on this page. Then fill in the missing words using the correct form of each word.

---

dominate *(verb)*

- dominance *(noun)*
  The dominance of the Roman Empire lasted more than a thousand years.

- dominant *(adjective)*
  The economy was the dominant issue for many voters in the last election.

maintain *(verb)*

- maintenance *(noun)*
  Marvin is responsible for the maintenance of all the computers and printers.

substantial *(adjective)*

- substantially *(adverb)*
  After a few months of lifting weights, Gina was substantially stronger than before.

---

1. Cell phones have _____ changed the way people communicate.

2. Microsoft Corporation has been a _____ force in technology.

3. What is essential for the _____ of good health?

4. The popularity of the World Cup is evidence of the _____ of soccer throughout the world.

5. A _____ number of jobs were eliminated by the closing of the factory.

Complete the paragraph using the correct forms of the five vocabulary words in this lesson. Each form of a word is used only once.

The Wild West

The Wild West refers to the American West from the end of the Civil War (1865) to the

early 20th century. Criminals and gangs of outlaws _____ parts of the

6.

West. Frequent bank and train robberies created _____ fear among

7.

ordinary people. The _____ of outlaws like Billy the Kid and Jesse James

8.

became legendary. It was difficult to _____ law and order. Many men did

9.

not want the role of sheriff. Their _____ interest was to stay alive. One

10.

_____ of this lawlessness was the need for each man to protect himself.

11.

This _____ explains why a man's gun was his most important possession.

12.

It takes a substantial commitment to maintain a positive family life.

What Do You Think?

Read each question and write a brief answer. Explain your answers in complete sentences.

1. Should maintaining peace in the family be the dominant rationale for family decisions?

   _____

   _____

   _____

2. Are the implications positive or negative for students who spend substantial amounts of time on the computer?

   _____

   _____

   _____

3. Should the potential to earn a substantial income be the dominant factor in choosing a job or career?

   _____

   _____

   _____

Reading Connection

Read the following passage. Answer the questions using complete sentences.

Human Memory

Do you remember what you had for breakfast this morning? Can you remember the name of your first teacher? Human memory stores information for a few seconds, a day, or a lifetime. Although scientists are not exactly sure how memory works, they know that several parts of the brain are involved in the process of remembering something. They believe that the three types of memory—sensory, short-term, and long-term—are connected.

Sensory memory

Information comes into the brain through the five senses. In less than a second, the brain decides which information is important to remember. For example, the bus driver sees a red light ahead. The brain determines that the information is important and passes it on to the short-term memory.

Short-term memory

Short-term memory is like a note pad where we write down the

things we want to remember. Short-term memory lets us remember what we read at the top of the page or what the teacher said a minute ago. The image of the red light is in the bus driver's short-term memory. It will disappear quickly, however, unless the brain connects the red light with information already stored in long-term memory.

Long-term memory

Long-term memory is where events and experiences are stored. Ideas, skills, and facts, including the meanings of words, are also in long-term memory. Information in long-term memory can last a lifetime (like the name of your first teacher). The bus driver has had many experiences with red lights, all of which are stored in long-term memory. Consequently, the driver remembers that a red light is a traffic signal that means to stop.

Memory plays a crucial role in the life of a human being.

1. Does short-term memory have a role in maintaining our interest in what we read? How?

   _____

   _____

2. Explain how the bus driver's memory puts the red light into a context.

   _____

   _____

3. Age and disease can cause substantial memory loss. What are some implications of memory loss?

   _____

   _____

context furthermore anticipate ambiguous
impose submit **dominate** aspect extent
implication pursue generate diverse
integral illustrate **maintain** standard
underlying **substantial** subsequent submit

New Word List

☐ context

☐ dominate

☐ implication

☐ maintain

☐ substantial

Review Word List

☐ _____

☐ _____

☐ _____

☐ _____

☐ _____

Writing Connection

Write a brief response to each question. Use words from this lesson or previous lessons in your answer. Write your answers in complete sentences.

Your niece just started high school and is having a difficult time making and keeping friends. Give her advice on how to maintain a friendship. Use specific examples from your own experience.

_____

_____

_____

_____

_____

How critical is it to have health insurance? What are the implications of not having health insurance? Give specific examples to support your answer.

_____

_____

_____

_____

_____

Reflection

Think about the words you have studied in this lesson.

1. Which words did you enjoy learning? _____

2. Select one word and imagine where you will use the word. Explain the situation.

_____

_____

3. Which words do you still need help with? _____

4. Return to the Knowledge Rating Chart at the beginning of this lesson. Complete column 3. How have your responses changed?

furthermore context anticipate illustrate
submit dominate substantial **impose** extent
implication **pursue** generate submit diverse
integral ambiguous maintain **standard**
aspect **subsequent** underlying submit

Vocabulary Knowledge Rating Chart

How well do you know the words? Use the numbers to rate your knowledge of the vocabulary words. Follow the teacher's directions.

4 = I know the word. I know it well enough to teach it to someone else.
3 = The word is familiar. I think I know what it means.
2 = I have heard the word, but I'm not sure what it means.
1 = I don't know the word at all.

	My rating before instruction	I think the word means	My rating after instruction
furthermore			
impose			
pursue			
standard			
subsequent			

Word Meaning Chart

Complete the chart. Follow the teacher's directions.

furthermore *(adverb)* /FUR ther mohr/ — **Furthermore** means in addition to.

EXAMPLES

The strong winds damaged the roof. _____, they blew over several trees.

Class Example: _____

My Example: Ms. Mitchell is an excellent teacher. **Furthermore,** _____

impose *(verb)* /im POHZ/ — To **impose** is to demand, require, or force people to accept or to do something.

EXAMPLES

The judge _____ the maximum penalty because of the seriousness of the crime.

Class Example: _____

My Example: The town **imposed** a ban on _____

pursue *(verb)* /per SOO/ — To **pursue** is to try to achieve something.

EXAMPLES

Until his death in 1968, Martin Luther King Jr. _____ justice and equality for all people.

Class Example: _____

My Example: After I get my diploma or GED credential, it is my intention to **pursue** _____

_____

standard *(noun)* /STAN derd/ — A **standard** is a required level of quality, ability, or skill.

EXAMPLES

Car safety _____ are designed to protect drivers and passengers.

Class Example: _____

My Example: High **standards** of skill are required for _____

subsequent *(adjective)* /SUHB si kwuhnt/ — **Subsequent** means that something comes after something else.

EXAMPLES

Unit 1 explains addition. _____ units explain subtraction, multiplication, and division.

Class Example: _____

My Example: **Subsequent** to winning the lottery, Brian _____

Exercise 1 Use the Words

Complete each sentence. Write the correct form of the vocabulary word in the blank space.

1. The goal of the diplomatic meetings was to _____ a peaceful solution to the border conflict.

2. A drug store robbery occurred last week. In the _____ investigation, the police identified a suspect.

3. The city library reduced its hours because of budget cuts. _____, the librarians were asked to take a pay cut.

4. Is it fair to _____ higher fines on drivers who do not have a valid license?

5. The Clean Air Act of 1990 set minimum national air-quality _____.

Exercise 2 Complete the Sentences

These sentences have been started for you. They are not complete. Complete them with your own words.

1. Subsequent to an argument with a friend or family member, I usually _____

_____

_____

2. When people try to impose their ideas on me, _____

_____

_____

3. Sports teach children discipline. Furthermore, _____

_____

_____

4. A standard of behavior for children is _____

_____

_____

5. If I had the time and money, I would pursue my dream of _____

_____

_____

Exercise 3 | Words at Work

Circle the best answer to each multiple choice question below. Then write a brief response to the question that follows. Write your answers in complete sentences.

1. The city bus company posted new hiring standards on its website last month. What should Sergei do before he sends in his resumé and application?

   (A) send in his resumé despite the new standards

   (B) review his resumé to make sure he meets the new standards

   (C) send in the application without his resumé

   What might be one of the new hiring standards? _____

   _____

   _____

2. Maritza and her friends often have lunch at the Home Grill Café because they work nearby. Subsequent to serving them their lunch orders, what does the server bring to the table?

   (A) water   **(B)** silverware   **(C)** dessert

   Subsequent to serving them lunch, what else does a server do? _____

   _____

   _____

3. The school Rachel attends imposed a dress code for the new school year. Furthermore, the code explicitly states that no student is excluded from following the code. Rachel does not like the new code. What is her best option?

   (A) wear whatever she wishes **(B)** follow the dress code

   (C) follow the dress code on most days

   Describe an experience when something was imposed on you that you did not like. _____

   _____

   _____

4. Jonathan is determined to pursue a career in healthcare. He is interested in becoming an ultrasound technician. What kind of information does Jonathan need to pursue his career goal?

   (A) the training requirements **(B)** the shift schedule at the local hospital

   (C) the names of clinics with ultrasound equipment

   What other information does Jonathan need to pursue his career goal? _____

   _____

   _____

Exercise 4 Word Families

Most words are part of a family of words. Study the word families on this page. Then fill in the missing words using the correct form of each word.

---

impose *(verb)*
• imposition *(noun)* Many people opposed the imposition of a higher sales tax.

pursue *(verb)*
• pursuit *(noun)* The pursuit of liberty is a crucial right mentioned in the Declaration of Independence.

subsequent *(adjective)*
• subsequently *(adverb)* After four years in the U.S. Senate, Barack Obama was subsequently elected president of the United States.

1. In a democracy, people use the legal system to _____ justice.

2. After the devastating hurricane, the _____ of a curfew prevented looting in the city.

3. The debate team won the regional competition and _____ won the state championship.

4. Is the _____ of profit the only rationale for starting a business?

5. To _____ higher bus fares would be a hardship for many riders.

Complete the paragraph using the correct forms of the five vocabulary words in this lesson. Each form of a word is used only once.

The U.S. Census

The _____ of fair government is demonstrated in many ways. One
       6.

way is the census, which is _____ on the country every 10 years. This
                              7.

_____ is required by the U.S. Constitution. The government must
      8.

_____ the goal of counting every person living in the country. People do
      9.

not have to meet a _____ to be counted in the census. After the census is
                        10.

complete, the data is _____ used to determine the number of seats each
                          11.

state has in the U.S. House of Representatives. _____, federal money is
                                                      12.

distributed according to the census data.

Are people judged by different standards because of their roles?

Exercise 5 What Do You Think?

Read each question and write a brief answer. Explain your answers in complete sentences.

1. Should higher moral standards be imposed on police officers and elected officials, or should they meet the same standards as the average person?

   _____

   _____

   _____

2. Subsequent to a serious conflict between two countries, should one country impose trade limitations on the other?

   _____

   _____

   _____

3. Are there negative or positive implications when a person continually pursues high personal standards?

   _____

   _____

Reading Connection

Read the following passage. Answer the questions using complete sentences.

Frequently Asked Questions about the GED® Tests

Every year, approximately 800,000 people in the United States, its territories, and Canada take the GED Tests. Although the GED certificate is not a high school diploma, it is accepted for admission to most colleges and universities. Below are some common questions about the GED Tests.

What does GED stand for?

GED stands for General Educational Development. The GED tests are a series of five tests. The tests measure the skills and knowledge that are similar to what is learned in high school.

What are the GED Tests?

There are five subject area tests: Reading, Language Arts (including an essay), Social Studies, Science, and Mathematics. The tests are multiple-choice and are timed. It takes about seven hours to complete all the tests.

Who qualifies to take the GED Tests?

A person may take the GED Tests if he or she
- is at least age 16 years old and not enrolled in high school.
- is not a high school graduate.
- meets other specific requirements within a particular state, territory, or province.

What skills do I need to pass the GED Tests?

To pass the GED Tests, a person must be able to read at the ninth-grade level, interpret information, and write clearly. The ability to add, subtract, multiply, and divide is necessary, along with basic knowledge of geometry and algebra.

For more information about GED testing, go to http://www.acenet.edu.

1. Suppose someone without a high school diploma wishes to go to a U.S. college or university. Will a GED certificate help the person pursue that goal? How?

   _____

   _____

2. Imagine you know a person who wants to take the GED Tests. She reads at a tenth-grade level. Furthermore, she writes clearly. Does that mean she is ready to take the tests? Explain.

   _____

   _____

3. Most employers impose hiring standards, such as a high school diploma or a GED certificate, on possible employees. What is the purpose of imposing these standards?

   _____

   _____

furthermore context anticipate illustrate
submit dominate substantial **impose** extent
implication **pursue** generate submit diverse
integral ambiguous maintain **standard**
aspect **subsequent** underlying submit

New Word List

- ☐ furthermore
- ☐ impose
- ☐ pursue
- ☐ standard
- ☐ subsequent

Review Word List

- ☐ _____
- ☐ _____
- ☐ _____
- ☐ _____
- ☐ _____

Exercise 7 # Writing Connection

Write a brief response to each question. Use words from this lesson or previous lessons in your answer. Write your answers in complete sentences.

The Declaration of Independence states that everyone has the right to the pursuit of happiness. How do you pursue your right? Do you pursue happiness the same way as your family or friends? Give specific examples.

_____

_____

_____

_____

_____

Your friend Elsa has high standards of behavior for her children. Is it acceptable for her to impose her standards on other people's children when they are guests in her home? Use specific examples to support your answer.

_____

_____

_____

_____

Exercise 8 # Reflection

Think about the words you have studied in this lesson.

1. Which words did you enjoy learning? _____

2. Select one word and imagine where you will use the word. Explain the situation.

_____

_____

3. Which words do you still need help with? _____

4. Return to the Knowledge Rating Chart at the beginning of this lesson. Complete column 3. How have your responses changed?

context furthermore **anticipate** ambiguous
aspect impose submit dominate extent
implication pursue generate **diverse** impose
illustrate **integral** maintain submit standard
underlying substantial subsequent **submit**

Vocabulary Knowledge Rating Chart

How well do you know the words? Use the numbers to rate your knowledge of the vocabulary words. Follow the teacher's directions.

4 = I know the word. I know it well enough to teach it to someone else.
3 = The word is familiar. I think I know what it means.
2 = I have heard the word, but I'm not sure what it means.
1 = I don't know the word at all.

	My rating before instruction	I think the word means	My rating after instruction
anticipate			
aspect			
diverse			
integral			
submit			

Word Meaning Chart

Complete the chart. Follow the teacher's directions.

anticipate *(verb)* /an TIS uh peyt/

To **anticipate** is to expect something to happen or to be ready for something to happen.

EXAMPLES

A good surgical nurse _____ the needs of the surgeon during an operation.

Class Example: _____

My Example: Get your tickets now because the concert organizers **anticipate** _____

aspect *(noun)* /AS pekt/

An **aspect** is a part of something, such as a plan, idea, or situation, that has many parts.

EXAMPLES

Lack of exercise can affect all _____ of a person's life, not just physical health.

Class Example: _____

My Example: There are many **aspects** to consider when making a decision _____

diverse *(adjective)* /dih VURS/

Diverse means different and widely varied.

EXAMPLES

Ben has a _____ music collection. It includes everything from jazz to hip-hop.

Class Example: _____

My Example: In my family, there are **diverse** points of view on _____

integral *(adjective)* /IN ti gruhl/

Integral tells that something is an essential and necessary part.

EXAMPLES

Because Mack Johnson dominates the defense, he is an _____ player on the team.

Class Example: _____

My Example: An **integral** ingredient in Italian food is _____

submit *(verb)* /suhb MIT/

To **submit** means to accept someone's authority or to agree to do something required or requested.

EXAMPLES

Olympic athletes must _____ to drug testing before the games begin.

Class Example: _____

My Example: I **submit** to having my backpack or purse searched when _____

Exercise 1 Use the Words

Complete each sentence. Write the correct form of the vocabulary word in the blank space.

1. The staff at the clinic was trained to meet the _____ needs of its clients.

2. What _____ of fractions do you need help with?

3. The airline gate agent announced, "We do not _____ any delays. All flights will depart on time."

4. The workers refused to _____ to the company's demands and went on strike.

5. During the American Revolution, the French played an _____ role in helping the colonists defeat the British.

Exercise 2 Complete the Sentences

These sentences have been started for you. They are not complete. Complete them with your own words.

1. One benefit of living in a culturally diverse community is _____

2. I anticipate having a good time when _____

3. An integral part of my childhood was _____

4. I would refuse to submit to _____

5. The aspect of being a student I like best is _____

Words at Work

Circle the best answer to each multiple choice question below. Then write a brief response to the question that follows. Write your answers in complete sentences.

1. The medical technicians at Parkway Medical Plaza often go out to lunch. They like to eat at The Lucky Dragon because its menu consists of diverse selections. What would you expect to see on The Lucky Dragon's diverse menu?

   (A) typical Chinese dishes   **(B)** soups and sandwiches   **(C)** different kinds of Asian foods

   What makes The Lucky Dragon's menu diverse? _____

   _____

2. At Redman's Cameras, all salespersons are expected to maintain the company's high standard of customer service. They should make every effort to anticipate customers' needs and questions. What is one way a salesperson can anticipate a customer's needs?

   (A) be prepared to explain the   **(B)** write down customers'   **(C)** organize products on
   features of each product   names   the shelves

   What is another way to anticipate a customer's needs or questions? _____

   _____

3. Cedric has applied for a security position at the airport. In the interview, he was told that all employees need to submit to a background check. Cedric wants the job, so he

   (A) specifies the information   **(B)** signs the form to give his   **(C)** requests a copy of the data.
   he will provide.   permission.

   Why does the security company require employees to submit to a background check? _____

   _____

4. Graciela is a single mother of three children. She was hired three months ago and is very happy with most aspects of her job. However, there is one aspect that pleases her most. What is it?

   (A) She gets a substantial   **(B)** She has flexibility in her   **(C)** She does not have to wear
   lunch break.   schedule.   a uniform.

   What aspect of a job is most important to you? _____

   _____

Word Families

Most words are part of a family of words. Study the word families on this page. Then fill in the missing words using the correct form of each word.

---

anticipate *(verb)*

• **anticipation** *(noun)*
  The residents bought extra food and batteries in anticipation of the storm.

submit *(verb)*

• **submission** *(noun)*
  A bully at school tries to force weaker students into submission.

• **submissive** *(adjective)*
  Fear can turn strong people into submissive individuals.

diverse *(adjective)*

• **diversity** *(noun)*
  The diversity of the students was one of his criteria for selecting a school.

• **diversify** *(verb)*
  To increase sales, the company decided to diversify its products.

---

1. The loan officer asked Lupe to _____ to a credit check.

2. It is time to _____ your film library. I am tired of watching action movies.

3. The _____ of going to Disneyland made the children excited and unable to sleep.

4. What data supports the theory that _____ in the workplace increases productivity?

5. The _____ clerk would not act without speaking to the manager.

Complete the paragraph using the correct forms of the five vocabulary words in this lesson. Each form of a word is used only once.

Ellen Ochoa

Ellen Ochoa is an inventor, a pilot, and the first female Hispanic astronaut. She is a woman

of _____ talents. She originally _____ pursuing
              6.   **7.**

a career in music. The _____ of her interests included math and science,
                            8.

so she studied physics and engineering. She did not _____ to the idea
                                                          9.

that women could not be astronauts. Now, Ellen speaks to students about the importance of

education. She enjoys this _____ of her job very much.
                               10.

In what ways do students benefit from diversity in the schools?

Exercise 5   What Do You Think?

Read each question and write a brief answer. Explain your answers in complete sentences.

1. What aspect of diversity at school is the most important for students to experience—diverse ideas and beliefs or diverse classmates and teachers?

   _____

   _____

   _____

2. Does the anticipation of problems play a more integral role in being a waiter or a babysitter?

   _____

   _____

   _____

3. Is submission to a person or an idea ever a positive action? What aspect of submission makes it a negative or positive experience?

   _____

   _____

Reading Connection

Read the following passage. Answer the questions using complete sentences.

The Navajo Code Talkers

Can words be secret weapons? During World War II, the United States was fighting Japan. In wartime, secure communication is crucial. The Japanese had a well-trained group of soldiers who spoke English. Therefore, they could easily understand American military radio communications.

A man named Philip Johnston thought that Navajo, a Native American language, could be used as a code to send radio messages that the Japanese army could not understand. Johnston grew up on a Navajo reservation as the son of a missionary. He spoke Navajo. The language does not have a written form. It is a tonal language and very difficult to learn. He also knew that Choctaw, another Native American language, had been used in World War I as a code.

In 1942, Johnston took his idea to the U.S. military. Within a few months, the first Navajo men joined the Marines. They developed a secret code using Navajo words and became known as the Code Talkers.

Some code words represented letters of the English alphabet. The Navajo word *be-la-sana* means ant and represented the letter A. The Code Talkers could spell out English words using a series of Navajo words.

Other Navajo words represented specific military terms. For example, the translation of *besh-lo* is iron fish, so the Code Talkers used it to mean submarine. They used *dah-he-tih-hi*, which means hummingbird, for fighter plane.

All together, about 400 Code Talkers sent and received thousands of messages during the war. The Japanese were never able to understand the code. The code remained a military secret for many years. Finally, in 1992, the Code Talkers were honored by the U.S. government for their service to the country during the war.

1. Explain how the Navajo Code Talkers had an integral military role in World War II.

_____

_____

2. What aspects of Philip Johnston's life allowed him to anticipate the fact that the Navajo language would make a good secret code?

_____

_____

3. How did the Navajo soldiers respond to the US government's request? Do you think they submitted willingly? Why?

_____

_____

context furthermore **anticipate** ambiguous **aspect** impose submit dominate extent implication pursue generate **diverse** impose illustrate **integral** maintain submit standard underlying substantial subsequent **submit**

New Word List

☐ anticipate

☐ aspect

☐ diverse

☐ integral

☐ submit

Review Word List

☐ _____

☐ _____

☐ _____

☐ _____

☐ _____

Exercise 7 Writing Connection

Write a brief response to each question. Use words from this lesson or previous lessons in your answer. Write your answers in complete sentences.

Some people cannot live without music, sports, or religion. What is integral to your life? Explain why it is integral and how it affects you. Give a specific example.

_____

_____

_____

_____

_____

Identify a job or career that interests you. What aspect of it do you find the most interesting? What aspect would be challenging? What aspect would be easy for you? Be specific.

_____

_____

_____

_____

_____

Exercise 8 Reflection

Think about the words you have studied in this lesson.

1. Which words did you enjoy learning? _____

2. Select one word and imagine where you will use the word. Explain the situation.

_____

_____

3. Which words do you still need help with? _____

4. Return to the Knowledge Rating Chart at the beginning of this lesson. Complete column 3. How have your responses changed?

context furthermore **ambiguous** anticipate

impose   submit   dominate   aspect   **extent**

implication **generate** pursue diverse

integral maintain **illustrate** standard

underlying substantial subsequent submit

Vocabulary Knowledge Rating Chart

How well do you know the words? Use the numbers to rate your knowledge of the vocabulary words. Follow the teacher's directions.

4 = I know the word. I know it well enough to teach it to someone else.
3 = The word is familiar. I think I know what it means.
2 = I have heard the word, but I'm not sure what it means.
1 = I don't know the word at all.

	My rating before instruction	I think the word means	My rating after instruction
ambiguous			
extent			
generate			
illustrate			
underlying			

Word Meaning Chart

Complete the chart. Follow the teacher's directions.

ambiguous *(adjective)* /am BIG yoo uhs/

Ambiguous tells that something may have more than one meaning or is not clear.

EXAMPLES

We could not draw any conclusions from the survey because the results were _____.

Class Example: _____

My Example: When I get an **ambiguous** response to a question, I feel _____

extent *(noun)* /ik STENT/

Extent is the size, amount, or importance of something.

EXAMPLES

The news photos revealed that the _____ of flooding was greater than anticipated.

Class Example: _____

My Example: Something or someone I rely on to a great **extent** is _____

generate *(verb)* /JEN uh reyt/

To **generate** is to produce or make something or cause something to happen.

EXAMPLES

Moises works two jobs in order to _____ sufficient income to support his family.

Class Example: _____

My Example: Teachers can **generate** interest in a subject by _____

illustrate *(verb)* /IL uh streyt/

To **illustrate** is to make meaning clear using examples or pictures, or to serve as an example.

EXAMPLES

A bar graph can _____ the changes in world population over the last century.

Class Example: _____

My Example: An example that **illustrates** our reliance on computers is _____

underlying *(adjective)* /UHN der lahy ing/

Underlying means the most basic, important, or fundamental.

EXAMPLES

In some countries, poor nutrition is the _____ cause of serious disease.

Class Example: _____

My Example: The **underlying** reason Nina did not pass the test was _____

Exercise 1 Use the Words

Complete each sentence. Write the correct form of the vocabulary word in the blank space.

1. Brainstorming is a strategy writers and students use to _____ ideas.

2. Politicians often make _____ statements about controversial issues because they do not want to lose votes.

3. What was the city council's _____ reason for prohibiting the sale of beer at the sports stadium?

4. The imposition of water rationing _____ how critical the drought has become.

5. Moving to another city meant that Noah would lose contact with his family and friends

   to some _____.

Exercise 2 Complete the Sentences

These sentences have been started for you. They are not complete. Complete them with your own words.

1. The extent of the damage to Richard's car meant that _____

   _____

   _____

2. The presence of graffiti illustrates the fact that _____

   _____

   _____

3. Because the instructions were ambiguous, I _____

   _____

   _____

4. When a child has consistent problems in school, a parent's underlying concern may be _____

   _____

   _____

5. When sports fans want to generate enthusiasm for their team, _____

   _____

   _____

Exercise 3 Words at Work

Circle the best answer to each multiple choice question below. Then write a brief response to the question that follows. Write your answers in complete sentences.

1. Chandra worked for Frazier Auto Parts for two years. According to her manager, she seemed to enjoy her job. Her manager was quite surprised when he learned that Chandra had applied for a job with another company. What could be the underlying reason Chandra applied for another job?

   (A) She did not like auto parts.

   (B) She did not get along with her manager.

   (C) She felt there were no advancement opportunities.

   What is another possible underlying reason Chandra applied for a different job? _____

   _____

   _____

2. Downtown Plastics imposed shift changes on all employees because of an increase in product orders. To what extent did the changes affect employees?

   (A) They worked longer hours. **(B)** They worked fewer hours. **(C)** They worked less overtime.

   To what extent would a schedule change at work or school affect you? _____

   _____

3. Danielle conducts a monthly orientation for new sales staff at a major department store. At the orientation, she shows a short video that consists of actual encounters between customers and sales clerks. What concept does the video illustrate for the new employees?

   (A) the importance of arriving on time

   (B) the importance of work schedules

   (C) the importance of good customer service

   What are two additional work concepts Danielle could illustrate at an orientation? _____

   _____

   _____

4. The owners of Coral Villas Retirement Home posted a memo on the bulletin board about changes in several staff positions. The memo generated a great deal of confusion and worry among employees and residents. Why did that happen?

   (A) The memo was explicit.

   (B) The memo was substantial.

   (C) The memo was ambiguous.

   How could the owners reverse the feelings generated by the memo? _____

   _____

   _____

Word Families

Most words are part of a family of words. Study the word families on this page. Then fill in the missing words using the correct form of each word.

extent *(noun)*
• extensive *(adjective)*   The apartment needed extensive repairs, so we did not rent it.

generate *(verb)*
• generation *(noun)*   Solar panels provide an alternative method for the generation of energy.

illustrate *(verb)*
• illustration *(noun)*   The children's story Pinocchio *is an* illustration *of the consequences of lying.*

underlying *(adjective)*
• underlie *(verb)*   Commitment and good study skills underlie student success.

1. Recent cases of food poisoning are an _____ of the need for stricter food safety regulations.

2. The _____ of new sales is the responsibility of all employees.

3. Last July, an _____ area of the country experienced a heat wave.

4. A lack of interest in the election seemed to _____ the low number of voters.

5. What is the _____ of China's influence on the global economy?

Complete the paragraph using the correct forms of the five vocabulary words in this lesson. Each form of a word is used only once.

The Writing Process

Good writers follow five steps that _____ a successful writing
                                              6.
process. The first step, prewriting, is the _____ of ideas. The writer then
                                                  7.
decides which ideas support the topic and which ideas _____ the
                                                           8.
important points. Next, the writer organizes these ideas and writes a first draft. In the third

step, changes are made to clarify anything that is _____. An example may
                                                         9.
be changed to provide a better _____ of a point. The writer may make
                                      10.
_____ changes. Finally, spelling and punctuation mistakes are corrected. It
        11.
takes hard work to _____ good writing.
                          12.

Scientists collect data on ocean temperatures and glaciers to determine the extent of global warming.

What Do You Think?

Read each question and write a brief answer. Explain your answers in complete sentences.

1. Is the extent of our understanding of global warming sufficient to generate changes in government policies or regulations?

   _____

   _____

   _____

2. Is there usually an underlying reason for a person to say or write something that is ambiguous?

   _____

   _____

   _____

3. What would generate more public interest and better illustrate the issue of world hunger—a television program or a celebrity who visits several poor countries?

   _____

   _____

Reading Connection

Read the following passage. Answer the questions using complete sentences.

The Federal Budget

The federal budget is the government's spending plan for the year. Every year, the U.S. president submits a budget to Congress. The House of Representatives and the Senate discuss the budget. During this process, changes are made to the budget. After Congress agrees on the budget changes, the budget is sent back to the White House for the president's signature.

FEDERAL BUDGET
1 **Defense and security: 23%** ($895 billion)
2 **Social Security: 20%** ($730 billion)
3 **Medicare & Medicaid: 21%** ($788 billion)
4 **Interest: 7%** ($251 billion)
5 **Education: 3%** ($115 billion)
6 **Science & Medical Research: 2%** ($76 billion)
7 **Veterans Benefits: 7%** ($251 billion)
8 **Other: 17%** ($612 billion)

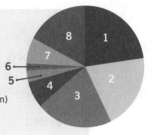

One of the crucial arguments is the amount of the budget. In 2010, it was almost $4 trillion ($4,000,000,000,000). The problem is that the U.S. government only collects about $2.5 trillion from taxes. Therefore, the government has to borrow more than $1 trillion to pay for everything in the budget. Consequently, the government pays interest on the borrowed money. The interest is substantial—more than $250 billion every year.

The federal budget pays for national defense, Social Security, Medicare, and programs like food stamps. Federal money also pays for the construction and repair of some bridges and roads, for medical and scientific research, and for some job training programs. The government also gives money to the states to help pay for education.

The pie chart shows what percentage of the federal budget is used to pay for different programs and services.

1. How much income does the U.S. government generate from taxes?

_____

_____

_____

2. To what extent are programs like Medicare and Social Security part of the federal budget?

_____

_____

_____

3. How does the pie chart illustrate the spending priorities of the U.S. government?

_____

_____

_____

context furthermore **ambiguous** anticipate
impose submit dominate aspect **extent**
implication **generate** pursue diverse
integral maintain **illustrate** standard
underlying substantial subsequent submit

New Word List

☐ ambiguous

☐ extent

☐ generate

☐ illustrate

☐ underlying

Review Word List

☐ _____

☐ _____

☐ _____

☐ _____

☐ _____

Exercise 7 # Writing Connection

Write a brief response to each question. Use words from this lesson or previous lessons in your answer. Write your answers in complete sentences.

Are the roles of men and women in American society today ambiguous? Use specific examples from your life to illustrate your opinion.

_____

_____

_____

_____

_____

Immigration is a topic that generates a lot of interest. Almost everyone agrees there is a need for reform. Describe a situation that illustrates a need for immigration reform. Try to use an example from your own experience if possible.

_____

_____

_____

_____

_____

Exercise 8 # Reflection

Think about the words you have studied in this lesson.

1. Which words did you enjoy learning? _____

2. Select one word and imagine where you will use the word. Explain the situation.

_____

_____

3. Which words do you still need help with? _____

4. Return to the Knowledge Rating Chart at the beginning of this lesson. Complete column 3. How have your responses changed?

Unit 3 Review

Activity 1 Make Statements and Questions

Write five statements or questions about the picture. Use one or more of the vocabulary words you studied in this unit in each sentence. You may also use words from previous units. <u>Underline</u> each vocabulary word you use.

Use this chart to choose different ways to make statements.

Make an observation:	Give an opinion:
There is/There are…	I think…
I notice that…	In my opinion/From my perspective…
It seems that…	It's important/It's essential…
Ask questions:	
Who, What, When, Where?	Do you think….?
Why, How, Which?	Is it important/Is it essential….?

Examples: In my opinion, airports need to <u>maintain</u> strict hiring <u>standards</u>.
Do you think children should have to <u>submit</u> to body searches?
Security checks often <u>generate</u> long lines for passengers.

_____

_____

_____

_____

_____

WORD BANK

AMBIGUOUS
ANTICIPATE
ASPECT
CONTEXT
DIVERSE
DOMINATE
EXTENT
FURTHERMORE
GENERATE
ILLUSTRATE
IMPLICATION
IMPOSE
INTEGRAL
MAINTAIN
PURSUE
STANDARD
SUBMIT
SUBSEQUENT
SUBSTANTIAL
UNDERLYING

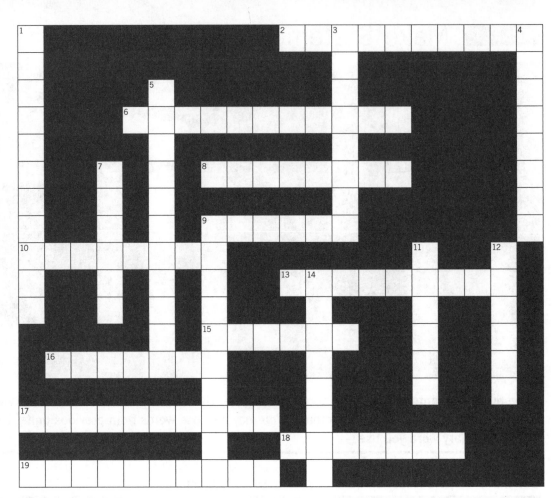

Activity 2 Puzzle

ACROSS

2. What are the _____ causes of racism?
6. A _____ number of students also work.
8. Hand washing is a health _____.
9. Is it necessary to _____ higher parking fees on weekends?
10. A pet is an _____ part of many families.
13. The _____ response upset the judge.
15. Travelers _____ to the laws of countries they visit.
16. What was the _____ of the complaint?
17. You can _____ long lines at the bank.
18. Ken's _____ interests include boxing and cooking.
19. If we are late, can we get seats on a _____ flight?

DOWN

1. What is the _____ of the new tax law for workers?
3. Women _____ most teaching staffs at elementary schools.
4. Will longer store hours _____ more sales?
5. The food at Al's Cafe is good. _____, the prices are reasonable.
7. Your attitude can determine the _____ of your happiness.
9. We need to _____ the importance of using seatbelts.
11. Why did Omar decide to _____ a business career?
12. What _____ of living in a large city do you like?
14. Vitamins help _____ good health.

Activity 3   Rewrite the Sentences

Use the correct forms of the vocabulary words from this unit to replace the underlined words. Underline all the vocabulary words you use.

Example: The young woman's answers were _unclear with several meanings,_ and she did not _continue to keep_ eye contact. _In addition_, she refused to _agree_ to a lie detector test.

The young woman's answers were <u>ambiguous,</u> and she did not <u>maintain</u> eye contact. <u>Furthermore</u>, she refused to <u>submit</u> to a lie detector test.

1. The producer _expected_ that the new movie would _produce large_ profits.

   _____

2. What are the _consequences_ of _trying to reach and achieve_ _very different_ goals at the same time?

   _____

3. The _basic and fundamental_ reason that the mayor's comment was _unclear_ and confusing was the fact that the reporter took the comment out of _the situation where they were said_.

   _____

Activity 4   Complete the Paragraph

Use the correct forms of the vocabulary words from this unit. Each word is used only once.

John Wooden

As a college basketball coach, John Wooden won the most games in college basketball

history. _____ coaches have been unable to break his record.
      1.

Wooden's UCLA team _____ the sport. Wooden's role as a teacher was
         2.

_____ to his effectiveness as a coach. He taught his players how to
   3.

_____ success on and off the court. This _____
   4.   **5.**

of his career is the _____ reason for his achievement. Wooden
        6.

_____ high _____ for himself and his players.
   7.   **8.**

He _____ discipline and _____ enthusiasm.
     9.   **10.**

_____, he _____ the fact that a person needs to live what
   11.   **12.**

he teaches. John Wooden died in 2010 and the age of 99.

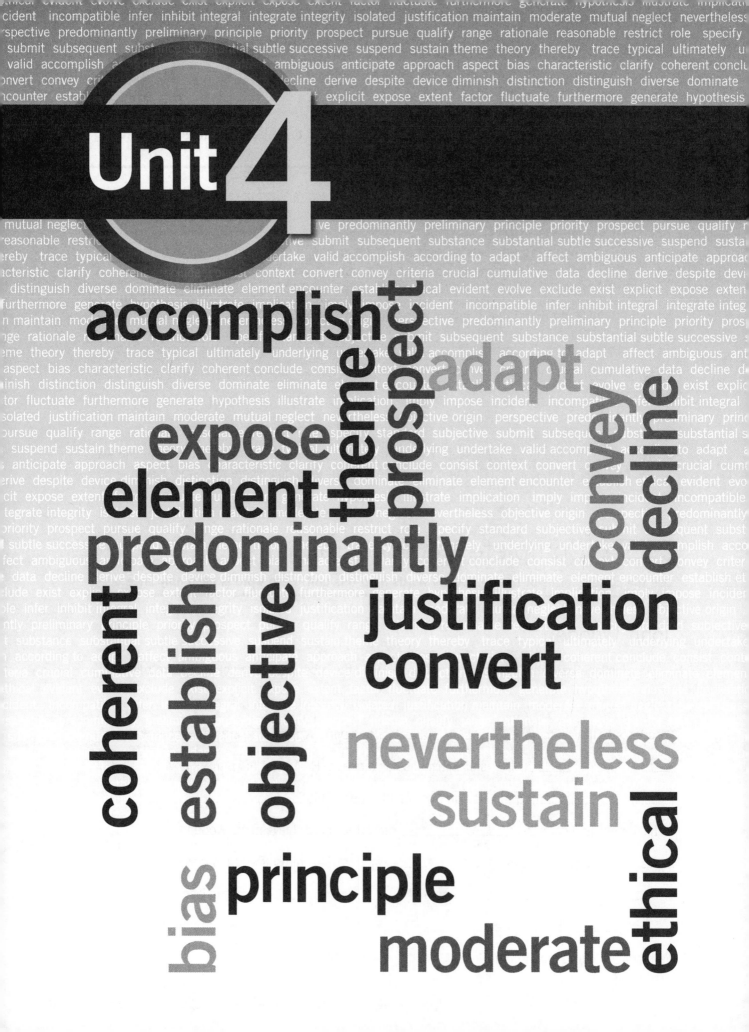

Unit 4

accomplish

theme prospect adapt

expose convey decline

element

predominantly

coherent establish objective justification

convert

nevertheless

sustain

bias principle ethical

moderate

bias coherent adapt accomplish principle
establish theme decline **convert** convey
objective **ethical** element bias justification
nevertheless moderate sustain **expose**
principle prospect theme predominantly

Vocabulary Knowledge Rating Chart

How well do you know the words? Use the numbers to rate your knowledge of the vocabulary words. Follow the teacher's directions.

4 = I know the word. I know it well enough to teach it to someone else.
3 = The word is familiar. I think I know what it means.
2 = I have heard the word, but I'm not sure what it means.
1 = I don't know the word at all.

	My rating before instruction	I think the word means	My rating after instruction
bias			
convert			
ethical			
expose			
principle			

Word Meaning Chart

Complete the chart. Follow the teacher's directions.

bias *(noun)* /BAHY uhs/

Bias is an attitude in favor of or against a person, group, thing, or belief.

EXAMPLES

The purpose of employment laws is to eliminate _____ in hiring practices in the workplace.

Class Example: _____

My Example: People who show **bias** for the home team include _____

---

convert *(verb)* /kuhn VURT/

To **convert** means to change something into a different form or function, or to change a belief or opinion.

EXAMPLES

At the airport in India, Jeremy can _____ his dollars into rupees.

Class Example: _____

My Example: After the earthquake, the government **converted** the school into a temporary _____

---

ethical *(adjective)* /ETH i kuhl/

Ethical tells that something or someone follows standards of right and wrong.

EXAMPLES

The candidate decided it was not _____ to accept large gifts from companies.

Class Example: _____

My Example: An **ethical** person does not _____

---

expose *(verb)* /ik SPOHZ/

To **expose** means to make something known, visible, or open to possible harm.

EXAMPLES

It is important to _____ children to art and music in school.

Class Example: _____

My Example: Jamal **exposed** the tattoo on his arm when _____

---

principle *(noun)* /PRIN suh puhl/

A **principle** is a truth, rule, or belief that is the basis for a theory, method, system, or behavior.

EXAMPLES

A basic economic _____ is that you should not spend more than you have.

Class Example: _____

My Example: The U.S. Constitution is based on **principles** such as religious freedom and _____

Exercise 1   Use the Words

Complete each sentence. Write the correct form of the vocabulary word in the blank space.

1. As a matter of _____, Josie did not make personal phone calls while she was babysitting.

2. Is it _____ to post pictures of someone online without her permission?

3. The mayor invited diverse members of the community to the meeting and announced,

    "Ethnic _____ has no place in our city."

4. The newspaper article on the front page _____ the illegal practices of the Adams Mortgage Company.

5. Green plants _____ sunlight into food and energy through the process of photosynthesis.

Exercise 2   Complete the Sentences

These sentences have been started for you. They are not complete. Complete them with your own words.

1. Justin felt that telling the truth was the ethical thing to do despite _____

    _____

    _____

2. One way to convert people from wasting energy to conserving it is _____

    _____

    _____

3. The referee demonstrated bias during the game by _____

    _____

    _____

4. I try not to expose feelings of anger when _____

    _____

    _____

5. Something that is against my principles is _____

    _____

    _____

Words at Work

Circle the best answer to each multiple choice question below. Then write a brief response to the question that follows. Write your answers in complete sentences.

1. Lorena works at Oakview Convalescent Center. A new policy states that employees have the option of converting unused sick days to regular pay at the end of the year. A maximum of five unused days is allowed. What is one reason for Lorena to convert unused sick days to regular paid time?

   (A) She might get sick.   **(B)** She needs to buy furniture.   **(C)** She will be able to work overtime.

   Would you convert your unused sick days or would you keep them for emergencies? Why?

   _____

2. Mr. Sanchez owns several apartment buildings. The downtown building needs many repairs. The tenants have also complained about the presence of pests, such as cockroaches. What action indicates that Mr. Sanchez is an ethical person?

   (A) He increases the rent.   **(B)** He paints the apartments.   **(C)** He makes the repairs quickly.

   What else can Mr. Sanchez do to demonstrate he is an ethical person? _____

   _____

3. Mabel works at Maywood Family Clinic. She came to work with a cold and a bad cough. Dr. Hart said, "Mabel, you sound terrible. Go home and rest, so you can get better faster. Furthermore, we do not want you to expose other employees or patients to your germs." What is the implication of exposing people to germs?

   (A) They might get sick.   **(B)** They will need to leave the clinic.   **(C)** They have to go to work.

   What can you do if you are exposed to the flu or a cold? _____

   _____

4. A poster in the employee lunchroom is titled *Principles of Success: Workplace Behavior*. A key principle is punctuality. Being on time for work is an illustration of this principle. What else illustrates this principle?

   (A) completing tasks on time   **(B)** taking time for breaks   **(C)** punching the time clock correctly

   Does this principle apply to students? Give a specific example. _____

   _____

   _____

Word Families

Most words are part of a family of words. Study the word families on this page. Then fill in the missing words using the correct form of each word.

---

bias *(noun)*

- biased *(adjective)*
  As the first black major league baseball player, Jackie Robinson encountered many biased athletes.

ethical *(adjective)*

- ethics *(noun)*
  Role models demonstrate excellence and ethics.
- ethically *(adverb)*
  Lawyers must act ethically with clients.

convert *(verb)*

- convertible *(adjective)*
  We bought a convertible sofa bed for the living room.
- conversion *(noun)*
  The conversion to a new computer system generated many problems.

expose *(verb)*

- exposure *(noun)*
  Exposure to second-hand smoke may cause lung cancer.

---

1. You can expect a mechanic with _____ to give you a fair price.

2. Is the _____ from metric to standard measurements simple?

3. Progress in medical technology has raised many _____ questions.

4. The Internet has given celebrities extensive media _____.

5. The reporter gave a _____ description of the mayor's speech.

Complete the paragraph using the correct forms of the five vocabulary words in this lesson. Each form of a word is used only once.

Principles of Emergency First Aid

The decision to respond in an emergency may be a reaction or an _____
                                                                          6.

response. The guiding _____ to remember is the need to determine
                            7.

danger. A rescuer should not _____ himself or herself to danger. Giving
                                    8.

first aid is based on three key principles of medical _____. First, always
                                                              9.

work to save life. Second, prevent the problem from getting worse. To stop bleeding, for

example, the rescuer may need to _____ a shirt into a bandage. Third,
                                        10.

begin efforts for recovery. There is no room in this process for _____.
                                                                        11.

All life is important.

Children are exposed to many different points of view.

Exercise 5 What Do You Think?

Read each question and write a brief answer. Explain your answers in complete sentences.

1. Does exposure to bias at an early age create biased adults?

   _____

   _____

   _____

2. Is it possible for criminals to be ethical and have moral principles?

   _____

   _____

   _____

3. Is it possible to convert biased individuals into tolerant people?

   _____

   _____

   _____

Reading Connection

Read the following passage. Answer the questions using complete sentences.

Japanese-American Relocation During World War II

On December 7, 1941, the Japanese bombed Pearl Harbor in Hawaii, and the United States went to war with Japan. The government did not trust the loyalty of Japanese-Americans. It forced 120,000 people of Japanese origin to move to relocation camps in isolated areas of the U.S. Two-thirds of the people were American citizens. Their basic rights were taken away, but they had broken no laws. Mary's letter describes her family's experience.

September 21, 1942

Dear Mrs. Turner,

We are finally settled in our "new home" at the relocation camp after a very long trip. When we got off the train, we were put in the back of a large truck. I was very worried about my mother. When we arrived at Manzanar, it was hot and dusty. The wind never seemed to stop blowing. I will never forget the shock we felt when we saw barbed wire around the entire camp and soldiers with guns standing at the gates!

I want to thank you again for storing several boxes of our family's possessions. We do not have to worry about our valuable keepsakes, especially the photo albums and my mother's tea set. You are a very kind and generous neighbor. It was a challenge to follow the directions we were given: Only pack what you can carry with your two hands.

I am so glad we packed many sheets, blankets, and towels. We are using the blankets as mattresses. They gave us beds but no mattresses. There was no other furniture, so my husband, George, and a few other men made us a table and a couple of chairs with some wood they found.

We are getting used to our new life. Our space in the barracks is very small, the size of one room. We use curtains to separate us from other families. We have no privacy and have to share bathrooms, showers, and eating areas. It is a real adjustment. However, we are happy that our family is together. We hope you are well.

Your former neighbor,
Mary Tanaka

1. Although it was legal for the government to force Japanese-Americans to leave their homes and move to relocation camps, was it ethical? Why or why not?

_____

2. How did bias play a role in the government's decision to relocate Mary and her family?

_____

3. There were many children in the camps. What kind of emotional impact could exposure to barbed wire fences and soldiers with guns have on them?

_____

bias coherent adapt accomplish principle establish theme decline **convert** convey objective **ethical** element bias justification nevertheless moderate sustain **expose** **principle** prospect theme predominantly

New Word List

☐ bias

☐ convert

☐ ethical

☐ expose

☐ principle

Review Word List

☐ _____

☐ _____

☐ _____

☐ _____

☐ _____

Writing Connection

Write a brief response to each question. Use words from this lesson or previous lessons in your answer. Write your answers in complete sentences.

Think of a person you know who has high moral principles. How does that person demonstrate that he or she is person of principle? Give a specific example to illustrate your answer.

_____

_____

_____

_____

_____

Imagine that you are on a committee working with the city council. The city received money to convert a vacant lot into something that will benefit the community. Should the lot be converted into a park, community garden, homeless shelter, or something else? Think about your community and what would benefit it the most.

_____

_____

_____

_____

Reflection

Think about the words you have studied in this lesson.

1. Which words did you enjoy learning? _____

2. Select one word and imagine where you will use the word. Explain the situation.

_____

_____

3. Which words do you still need help with? _____

4. Return to the Knowledge Rating Chart at the beginning of this lesson. Complete column 3. How have your responses changed?

bias **coherent** adapt theme convey

accomplish convert **establish** bias

ethical **objective** element justification

nevertheless expose moderate **sustain**

principle prospect **theme** predominantly

Vocabulary Knowledge Rating Chart

How well do you know the words? Use the numbers to rate your knowledge of the vocabulary words. Follow the teacher's directions.

4 = I know the word. I know it well enough to teach it to someone else.
3 = The word is familiar. I think I know what it means.
2 = I have heard the word, but I'm not sure what it means.
1 = I don't know the word at all.

	My rating before instruction	I think the word means	My rating after instruction
coherent			
establish			
objective			
sustain			
theme			

Word Meaning Chart

Complete the chart. Follow the teacher's directions.

coherent *(adjective)* /koh HEER uhnt/

Coherent tells that something is clear, logical, and easy to understand.

EXAMPLES

_____ writing develops the writer's ideas logically and clearly.

Class Example: _____

My Example: Your directions were **coherent**, so _____

establish *(verb)* /ih STAB lish/

To **establish** means to start or create an organization, situation, relationship, or reputation.

EXAMPLES

The Rotary Club _____ a scholarship for students to attend community college.

Class Example: _____

My Example: I **established** a routine to _____

objective *(adjective)* /uhb JEK tiv/

Objective tells that something is based on facts and not on personal feelings or beliefs.

EXAMPLES

It is difficult for parents to be _____ when discussing their children.

Class Example: _____

My Example: A person who needs to be **objective** on the job is _____

sustain *(verb)* /suh STEYN/

To **sustain** means to keep something going or make it continue or last.

EXAMPLES

A marathon runner needs to _____ physical energy and mental focus.

Class Example: _____

My Example: In pursuing my goals, it is sometimes difficult to **sustain** _____

theme *(noun)* /theem/

A **theme** is the main subject or idea in a piece of writing, speech, movie, event, or decoration.

EXAMPLES

The _____ of the student's speech was the value of pursuing your dreams.

Class Example: _____

My Example: A **theme** I enjoy writing about is _____

Exercise 1 Use the Words

Complete each sentence. Write the correct form of the vocabulary word in the blank space.

1. Despite their differences, the two countries made every effort to _____ the trade talks.

2. Lost love has been a common _____ of songs and poems throughout time.

3. The police _____ a connection between the store robbery this week and the bank robbery last week.

4. Scientists need to be _____ when testing a hypothesis.

5. When the actress won the award, she was so excited that her thank-you speech was not

   _____ .

Exercise 2 Complete the Sentences

These sentences have been started for you. They are not complete. Complete them with your own words.

1. One way to sustain a friendship is _____

   _____

   _____

2. It is necessary for me to be objective when _____

   _____

   _____

3. An appropriate theme for a school program for parents of adolescents would be _____

   _____

   _____

4. I would like to establish a reputation for myself as _____

   _____

   _____

5. It is important to give a coherent explanation when _____

   _____

   _____

Words at Work

Circle the best answer to each multiple choice question below. Then write a brief response to the question that follows. Write your answers in complete sentences.

1. After numerous requests from employees, the owners of Logan Furniture Factory established a child-care center in the room next to the cafeteria. What is the underlying reason for their decision to establish a child-care center?

   (A) to prevent employees from leaving   **(B)** to eliminate overtime   **(C)** to attract and keep employees

   How does establishing a child-care center affect employees? _____

   _____

   _____

2. George sells washers and dryers at Central Appliances. He has established himself as a top salesperson at the store because of his friendly manner and coherent sales presentations. Why do customers appreciate his coherent presentations?

   (A) They are clear and easy to understand.   **(B)** They are short and ambiguous.   **(C)** They generate questions.

   How does a person prepare to give a coherent presentation? _____

   _____

   _____

3. Calvin and Alisa plan to open a seafood restaurant downtown. They are meeting with an interior designer next week to decide how to design and decorate the restaurant. The designer wants them to choose a theme. Which theme would work best for their restaurant?

   (A) a sea and mermaid theme   **(B)** a star and moon theme   **(C)** a dragon and fairy theme

   What restaurant has a theme you particularly like? Describe it. _____

   _____

4. Althea convinced her company to start a recycling program. Althea promised to sustain the program after it got started. What is one thing Althea can do to sustain recycling efforts at her work site?

   (A) bring plastic bottles to work   **(B)** put up notices to remind employees   **(C)** remove all trash cans

   What else can Althea do to sustain the recycling program? _____

   _____

Word Families

Most words are part of a family of words. Study the word families on this page. Then fill in the missing words using the correct form of each word.

---

coherent *(adjective)*
• coherently *(adverb)* *The witness coherently described the details of the accident to the police officer.*

establish *(verb)*
• establishment *(noun)* *The requirements for the establishment of residency are different in each state.*

objective *(adjective)*
• objectively *(adverb)* *Judges objectively listen to lawyers from both sides of a legal case.*

sustain *(verb)*
• sustainable *(adjective)* *Solar power is a form of sustainable energy.*

1. If workers want a _____ retirement, they will have to plan carefully.

2. The _____ of credit is a first step in becoming financially independent.

3. The hiring committee _____ reviewed the applicants' resumes.

4. Will water, nuts, and dried fruit be enough to _____ you on your hike?

5. A press secretary must be able to _____ answer questions on the spot.

6. Bill Gates and Paul Allen _____ Microsoft Corporation in 1976.

Complete the paragraph using the correct forms of the five vocabulary words in this lesson. Each form of a word is used only once.

The Environmental Protection Agency (EPA)

The _____ of the EPA (Environmental Protection Agency) in 1970,
  7.

was a result of public concern for the environment. The EPA is an independent federal agency

that protects and _____ the environment. It _____
  8. 9.

standards to control and eliminate pollution. Furthermore, it has the responsibility to

_____ enforce the standards. It does research and provides
  10.

information and _____ explanations about _____
  11. 12.

forms of energy. A clean and healthy environment is the responsibility of everyone.

This _____ underlies the work of the EPA.
  13.

Presidents and religious leaders often share perspectives.

Exercise 5 What Do You Think?

Read each question and write a brief answer. Explain your answers in complete sentences.

1. Is it possible for a religious leader, such as a minister, priest, or rabbi, to establish an objective perspective?

____

____

____

2. Can a person who is angry speak coherently and objectively?

____

____

____

3. Is it easier to establish trust or sustain trust in a relationship?

____

____

____

Read the following passage. Answer the questions using complete sentences.

The United States Constitution

In 1787, the United States was a new country with only 13 states. The federal government was weak and not very effective. A group of men from the states met in Philadelphia. Their purpose was to fix the government. Among them were George Washington, James Madison, Alexander Hamilton, and Benjamin Franklin.

From May to September, these men debated ideas for a more effective government. They decided that instead of fixing the government, they had to create a new plan for the government. The plan was called the Constitution. It outlined the basic laws and principles of the new American democracy. The meeting in Philadelphia became known as the Constitutional Convention; the men became known as the Framers of the Constitution.

The original Constitution consisted of two sections: the Preamble and the Articles. Later, the third section, a list of Amendments, was added as the Constitution was amended, or changed.

The Preamble, or introduction, is very short—only one sentence—and explains the rationale for the Constitution. It begins with the famous words, "We the people of the United States...."

The Articles create and define the three branches of the government: the legislative (Congress), the executive (the president and vice-president), and the judicial (the Supreme Court). The Articles specify the powers of each branch, the role of the states, and how the Constitution can be amended.

The first 10 amendments are called the Bill of Rights. They guarantee citizens certain rights, such as freedom of religion, freedom of speech, and the right to a speedy trial before a jury. Other important amendments include the 13th amendment, which ended slavery, and the 19th amendment, which gave women the right to vote. To date, the Constitution has been amended 27 times.

The Constitution is the supreme law of the land. Its principles underlie all state and federal laws.

1. Which part of the Constitution established the three branches of government?

2. The Framers anticipated the need for the Constitution to be relevant for each successive generation. How does the Constitution sustain its relevance for future generations?

3. Over 200 years ago, the Framers of the Constitution created a coherent plan for a government. Explain how the Constitution is a coherent plan. Give at least one example.

bias **coherent** adapt theme convey
accomplish convert **establish** bias
ethical **objective** element justification
nevertheless expose moderate **sustain**
principle prospect **theme** predominantly

New Word List

☐ coherent

☐ establish

☐ objective

☐ sustain

☐ theme

Review Word List

☐ _____

☐ _____

☐ _____

☐ _____

☐ _____

Exercise 7 # Writing Connection

Write a brief response to each question. Use words from this lesson or previous lessons in your answer. Write your answers in complete sentences.

Think of a favorite movie. Explain what the theme of the movie is and why you like the movie. Make sure your response is coherent.

_____

_____

_____

_____

_____

Your coworker Myra has asked for your advice. She had a problem with a previous neighbor. She wants to know how to establish a good relationship with the new neighbor who will be moving in next week. What advice do you have for her?

_____

_____

_____

_____

_____

Exercise 8 # Reflection

Think about the words you have studied in this lesson.

1. Which words did you enjoy learning? _____

2. Select one word and imagine where you will use the word. Explain the situation.

_____

_____

3. Which words do you still need help with? _____

4. Return to the Knowledge Rating Chart at the beginning of this lesson. Complete column 3. How have your responses changed?

bias   coherent   accomplish   **adapt**   convey

establish   **decline**   prospect   convert   convey

ethical   element   theme   **justification**

nevertheless   expose   sustain   submit

prospect   theme   bias   **predominantly**

Vocabulary Knowledge Rating Chart

How well do you know the words? Use the numbers to rate your knowledge of the vocabulary words. Follow the teacher's directions.

4 = I know the word. I know it well enough to teach it to someone else.
3 = The word is familiar. I think I know what it means.
2 = I have heard the word, but I'm not sure what it means.
1 = I don't know the word at all.

	My rating before instruction	I think the word means	My rating after instruction
adapt			
decline			
justification			
nevertheless			
predominantly			

Word Meaning Chart

Complete the chart. Follow the teacher's directions.

---

adapt *(verb)* /uh DAPT/

To **adapt** is to change or adjust something so it can be used for a different purpose or fit a different situation.

EXAMPLES

When he moved from Florida, James had to _____ to the cold climate of Canada.

Class Example: _____

My Example: Most students need time to **adapt** to _____

---

decline *(verb)* /dih KLAHYN/

To **decline** is to decrease in quantity, amount, importance, or quality.

EXAMPLES

In some cities, enrollments in public schools have _____.

Class Example: _____

My Example: Parents' influence begins to **decline** when their children _____

---

justification *(noun)* /juhs tuh fi KEY shuhn/

A **justification** is a reasonable explanation for something that may be questionable.

EXAMPLES

The need for more safety was the _____ for hiring extra security guards.

Class Example: _____

My Example: A **justification** for a classroom party is _____

---

nevertheless *(adverb)* /nev er thuh LES/

Nevertheless means however or despite something unexpected.

EXAMPLES

The forecast is for very hot weather. The graduation will take place outdoors _____.

Class Example: _____

My Example: After a day at school or work, I am usually tired. **Nevertheless,** _____

---

predominantly *(adverb)* /pri DOM uh nuhnt lee/ **Predominantly** means mostly or mainly.

EXAMPLES

Are the students in this class _____ male or female?

Class Example: _____

My Example: People in my neighborhood travel to school or work **predominantly** by _____

Exercise 1　Use the Words

Complete each sentence. Write the correct form of the vocabulary word in the blank space.

1. When did the dominance of the Roman Empire begin to _____?

2. Abraham Lincoln lost two elections to become an Illinois senator.

   _____, he became president of the United States.

3. "The barber's presence at the crime scene is sufficient _____ for his arrest," said the police chief.

4. At the time of the Civil War, the South's economy was _____ agricultural.

5. According to the theory of evolution, animals must _____ to their environment or they will cease to exist.

Exercise 2　Complete the Sentences

These sentences have been started for you. They are not complete. Complete them with your own words.

1. In my opinion, there is never a justification for _____

   _____

   _____

2. I have predominantly happy memories of _____

   _____

   _____

3. Something that can cause a person's health to decline is _____

   _____

   _____

4. When people get married, they have to adapt to _____

   _____

   _____

5. My cousin is quite shy. Nevertheless, _____

   _____

   _____

Exercise 3 Words at Work

Circle the best answer to each multiple choice question below. Then write a brief response to the question that follows. Write your answers in complete sentences.

1. Wilma works 20 hours per week as a customer service representative for a cable television company. Her manager told her that next month her hours will be reduced to 18 hours per week. What was the justification for the cut in hours?

   (A) A new computer system is able to handle some of the calls.

   (B) There are more customers calling for assistance.

   (C) The company is pleased with Wilma's work.

   What is another possible justification for cutting an employee's hours? _____

   _____

2. Damita uses a wheelchair. She needs assistance entering the building where she works because there are steps at the entrance. Damita asked the building management to adapt the entrance to allow her to enter on her own. How could the management adapt the entrance to meet Damita's request?

   (A) paint the doors a bright color

   (B) add a ramp to the entrance

   (C) hire somebody to open the door

   How else could the building management adapt the entrance for people with disabilities?

   _____

3. Milton is a bartender at a downtown hotel that serves predominantly foreign tourists. What aspect of working at this hotel does he most enjoy?

   (A) his encounters with people from different countries

   (B) washing the dirty glasses

   (C) wearing a hotel uniform

   What is a business you know that serves predominantly one type of customer? _____

   _____

4. The owner of Sammy's Barbecue Ribs & Burgers changed the menu. He eliminated the ribs and included pizza and salads. He noticed that his sales began to decline. What did the owner conclude?

   (A) Customers liked the menu changes.

   (B) Customers preferred the previous menu.

   (C) Customers did not notice the menu changes.

   What is another reason sales can decline at a restaurant? _____

   _____

   _____

Exercise 4 Word Families

Most words are part of a family of words. Study the word families on this page. Then fill in the missing words using the correct form of each word.

---

adapt *(verb)*

- adaptation *(noun)*
  I saw a film adaptation of the novel.

- adaptable *(adjective)*
  Children are highly adaptable to change.

decline *(verb)*

- decline *(noun)*
  Car sales are on the decline this year.

- declining *(adjective)*
  My aunt's declining health worried me.

justification *(noun)*

- justify *(verb)*
  How did Sam justify being late?

nevertheless *(adverb)*

- nonetheless *(adverb)*
  I left work early. Nonetheless, I was late.

predominantly *(adverb)*

- predominant *(adjective)*
  Red is the quilt's predominant color.

---

1. In his speech, the president tried to _____ the increase in spending.

2. Is the Internet responsible for the _____ number of daily newspapers?

3. To stay competitive, companies must be _____ to market changes.

4. The team lost five games. The coach has confidence in them _____.

5. Pollution has led to the _____ of some species of wildlife.

Complete the paragraph using the correct forms of the five vocabulary words in this lesson. Each form of a word is used only once.

The Decline of Tropical Rainforests

Tropical rainforests exist _____ in South America, Southeast Asia, and
                                    6.

Africa. Rainforest plants and animals have developed _____ to live in this
                                                              7.

environment. Many are not _____ to live elsewhere. Rainforests are crucial
                                  8.

to the global climate. _____, people _____ cutting
                              9.   **10.**

down portions of the forests for lumber. The _____ size of the rainforests
                                                      11.

is troubling. At one time, 6 million square miles of tropical rainforest existed. That number has

_____ to only 2.6 million.
12.

In a person's declining years, circumstances can change and affect the entire family.

Exercise 5 What Do You Think?

Read each question and write a brief answer. Explain your answers in complete sentences.

1. Which is easier for family members to adapt to—a loved one's declining health or declining memory?

   _____

   _____

2. Does achieving success require the ability to adapt to changing circumstances, or is it predominantly the result of luck?

   _____

   _____

3. Many experts say there is never a justification for physical punishment of children. Nevertheless, there are parents who spank their children. Can parents justify spanking their children?

   _____

   _____

   _____

Reading Connection

Read the following passage. Answer the questions using complete sentences.

Solar Eclipse—When Day Becomes Night

According to an ancient Chinese legend, a great dragon lived in the sky, and from time to time, it would swallow the sun. People believed the legend because it explained something they did not understand—a solar eclipse.

Solar refers to the sun. As the moon orbits the earth, it sometimes passes directly between the earth and the sun. The result is a solar eclipse. During an eclipse, the moon blocks the sun's light, causing a shadow to cover a section of the earth's surface. A solar eclipse can be either total or partial.

During a total eclipse, the sun's light is completely blocked by the moon. Only a halo of light is visible around the edge of the sun. The area of darkness caused by the moon's shadow is quite small; it may extend only 60 to 200 miles in width. A total eclipse may last about seven minutes. Total solar eclipses are rare—only about 70 occur during a century.

In a partial eclipse, the moon covers only a portion of the sun. Part of the sun is dark and part remains bright. The moon's shadow on the earth is larger, so a partial eclipse can be seen across a wider area than a total eclipse. A partial eclipse can last for an hour or longer.

Whether it is total or partial, a solar eclipse is one of nature's most spectacular events.

1. What is the role of the moon in a solar eclipse?

_____

_____

_____

2. Has there been a decline in the belief that dragons cause solar eclipses? If so, what has contributed to the decline?

_____

_____

_____

3. Is a solar eclipse interesting only to people who are predominantly scientists? Why would a solar eclipse interest other people as well?

_____

_____

_____

_____

bias coherent accomplish **adapt** convey
establish **decline** prospect convert convey
ethical element theme **justification**
nevertheless expose sustain submit
prospect theme bias **predominantly**

New Word List

☐ adapt

☐ decline

☐ justification

☐ nevertheless

☐ predominantly

Review Word List

☐ _____

☐ _____

☐ _____

☐ _____

☐ _____

Exercise 7 # Writing Connection

Write a brief response to each question. Use words from this lesson or previous lessons in your answer. Write your answers in complete sentences.

Is there ever a valid justification for war? What circumstances, if any, would justify the death and destruction caused by war?

_____

_____

_____

_____

_____

Many people believe that good manners and common courtesy have declined over the years. Is there a predominant reason for this decline?

_____

_____

_____

_____

_____

Exercise 8 # Reflection

Think about the words you have studied in this lesson.

1. Which words did you enjoy learning? _____

2. Select one word and imagine where you will use the word. Explain the situation.

_____

_____

3. Which words do you still need help with? _____

4. Return to the Knowledge Rating Chart at the beginning of this lesson. Complete column 3. How have your responses changed?

bias coherent adapt **accomplish** theme
establish prospect convert decline **convey**
ethical **element** convey objective adapt
nevertheless sustain **moderate** submit
prospect theme expose predominantly

Vocabulary Knowledge Rating Chart

How well do you know the words? Use the numbers to rate your knowledge of the vocabulary words. Follow the teacher's directions.

4 = I know the word. I know it well enough to teach it to someone else.
3 = The word is familiar. I think I know what it means.
2 = I have heard the word, but I'm not sure what it means.
1 = I don't know the word at all.

	My rating before instruction	I think the word means	My rating after instruction
accomplish			
convey			
element			
moderate			
prospect			

Word Meaning Chart

Complete the chart. Follow the teacher's directions.

accomplish *(verb)* /uh KOM plish/

To **accomplish** means to do or complete something successfully.

EXAMPLES

The team _____ its objective of winning more than 50 percent of its games.

Class Example: _____

My Example: When I **accomplish** a goal, I feel _____

convey *(verb)* /kuhn VEY/

To **convey** means to express or communicate a message, feeling, or information with or without words.

EXAMPLES

The teacher wants to _____ to her students that learning can be fun.

Class Example: _____

My Example: The photograph of the desert **conveys** a feeling of _____

element *(noun)* /EL uh muhnt/

An **element** is an essential or typical part of a whole system, plan, or piece of work.

EXAMPLES

Shooting and dribbling are _____ of basketball.

Class Example: _____

My Example: A key **element** of a healthy diet is _____

moderate *(adjective)* /MOD er it/

Moderate tells that something is not extreme but is average in amount, intensity, or degree.

EXAMPLES

The weather report predicts _____ to heavy rains this weekend.

Class Example: _____

My Example: A **moderate** amount of sleep for me is _____

prospect *(noun)* /PROS pekt/

A **prospect** is the possibility that something will happen.

EXAMPLES

The _____ of graduating in June encouraged Josette to work harder.

Class Example: _____

My Example: I get excited at the **prospect** of _____

Exercise 1 Use the Words

Complete each sentence. Write the correct form of the vocabulary word in the blank space.

1. Subjects and predicates are _____ of English grammar.

2. The _____ increase in bus fares did not significantly impact the use of public transportation.

3. In 1969, the U.S. space agency, NASA, _____ its mission of putting a man on the moon.

4. What is the _____ that the environmental meeting will establish stricter standards?

5. The ambassador attended the funeral and _____ the president's message of sympathy to the general's wife.

Exercise 2 Complete the Sentences

These sentences have been started for you. They are not complete. Complete them with your own words.

1. Love and friendship are key elements of happiness. Another element is _____

   _____

   _____

2. Parents convey to their children that _____

   _____

   _____

3. I can improve my job prospects by _____

   _____

   _____

4. A task I hope to accomplish this week is _____

   _____

   _____

5. People who drive at moderate speeds _____

   _____

   _____

Exercise 3 Words at Work

Circle the best answer to each multiple choice question below. Then write a brief response to the question that follows. Write your answers in complete sentences.

1. Stan wants to open a small lunch stand, Stan's Sandwich Stop, near several
    medical and office buildings. He did some research and studied the elements of
    the small lunch business. What is one of the elements of a successful lunch stand?

    (A) a colorful menu   **(B)** a children's menu   **(C)** moderate prices

    What is another element of a successful lunch stand? _____

    _____

    _____

2. Shireen has an interview for the position of receptionist at Goldstar Medical
    Group. She wants to convey to the interviewer that she has a positive attitude and
    the necessary skills to be a good receptionist. What can Shireen do during the
    interview to convey her qualities? She can

    (A) sit up and look down.   **(B)** smile often and speak   **(C)** laugh often and make jokes.
                                       coherently.

    What else can Shireen do to convey her abilities and attitude? _____

    _____

3. The managers at Stern Clothing Designs announced to the employees that their
    new catalog had generated unanticipated sales. As a result, the employees would
    have an opportunity to sign up for overtime hours. Employees would receive time
    and a half pay for each overtime hour. The prospect of working overtime made the
    employees feel

    (A) concerned.   **(B)** pleased.   **(C)** stressed.

    Do all employees feel the same at the prospect of working overtime? _____

    _____

4. The employees at AFG Paper Co. were required to attend a meeting to discuss
    increasing productivity. They learned that a person's ability to accomplish tasks
    declines with fatigue. Therefore, well-rested employees can accomplish more. Why
    is this?

    (A) They make fewer   **(B)** They don't distract   **(C)** They drink fewer cups
       mistakes.   coworkers by yawning.   of coffee.

    What is another reason a well-rested person can accomplish more? _____

    _____

Word Families

Most words are part of a family of words. Study the word families on this page. Then fill in the missing words using the correct form of each word.

---

accomplish *(verb)*

- accomplishment *(noun)*
  It is a major accomplishment to earn a diploma while working full time.

- accomplished *(adjective)*
  Manuel is an accomplished guitar player.

---

moderate *(adjective)*

- moderately *(adverb)*
  Riding a motorcycle in traffic may be moderately dangerous.

- moderation *(noun)*
  It is best to exercise in moderation.

---

prospect *(noun)*

- prospective *(adjective)*
  Prospective tenants need to provide references and credit information.

---

1. The instructions were _____ helpful, but we still had questions.

2. Lawyers question all _____ jurors before selecting a jury.

3. Did the _____ earthquake cause much damage to the town?

4. Yvonne felt a sense of _____ after the marathon.

5. _____ in eating and drinking helped Gordon maintain his weight.

Complete the paragraph using the correct forms of the five vocabulary words in this lesson. Each form of a word is used only once.

The Williams Sisters

Venus and Serena Williams are two of the most _____ women

6.

tennis players in the world. They are also sisters. Their many _____

7.

on the tennis court have made them famous. _____ opponents know

8.

they will encounter power and speed when they play Venus or Serena. The sisters have also

_____ much off the tennis court. Venus and Serena have both studied the

9.

_____ of fashion design. As a result, they design their own outfits for

10.

tennis tournaments. Their fashions _____ their personalities—unique,

11.

stylish, and very individualistic.

Trust and cooperation are essential elements of a healthy relationship.

What Do You Think?

Read each question and write a brief answer. Explain your answers in complete sentences.

1. Should prospective marriage partners analyze the key elements of successful relationships?

    _____

    _____

    _____

2. Should parents convey the pride they feel in their children's accomplishments to other people?

    _____

    _____

    _____

3. Can pursuing a life of moderation produce great accomplishments?

    _____

    _____

    _____

Reading Connection

Read the following passage. Answer the questions using complete sentences.

A Doll's House

In Europe in the late 1800s, men and women had very traditional roles in society and marriage. Women stayed home, raised the children, and followed the wishes of their husbands. A Doll's House is a play written by Henrik Ibsen, a Norwegian playwright, in 1879. In A Doll's House, Ibsen sharply criticizes these traditional marriage roles. The play was very controversial when it was published. The format of a play is different from other literature. A play script consists predominantly of the characters' dialogue and actions. There is very little, if any, description of what the characters are thinking or feeling. The reader must make inferences based on what the characters say to each other. In the passage below, Nora expresses her feelings to her husband, Torvald Helmer.

NORA: [*shaking her head*] You never loved me. You've thought it fun to be in love with me, that's all.

HELMER: Nora, what a thing to say!

NORA: Yes, it's true, Torvald. When I lived at home with Papa, he told me all his opinions, so I had the same ones too; or if they were different I hid them, since he wouldn't have cared for that. He used to call me his doll-child, and he played with me the way I played with my dolls. Then I came into your house—

HELMER: How can you speak of our marriage like that?

NORA: [*unperturbed*] I mean, then I went from Papa's hands into yours. You arranged everything to your own taste, and so I got the same taste as you—or I pretended to; I can't remember. I guess a little of both, first one, then the other. Now when I look back, it seems as if I'd lived like a beggar—just from hand to mouth. I've lived by doing tricks for you, Torvald. But that's the way you wanted it. It's a great sin what you and Papa did to me. You're to blame that nothing's become of me.

HELMER: Nora, how unfair and ungrateful you are! Haven't you been happy here?

NORA: No, never. I thought so—but I never have.

1. What feelings does Nora convey to her husband, Torvald?

_____

2. Are there elements in Nora's relationship with Torvald that are similar to her relationship with her father? Explain.

_____

_____

3. Based on what Nora says to her husband, what do you think are the prospects for their marriage?

_____

_____

bias coherent adapt **accomplish** theme
establish prospect convert decline **convey**
ethical **element** convey objective adapt
nevertheless sustain **moderate** submit
prospect theme expose predominantly

New Word List

☐ accomplish

☐ convey

☐ element

☐ moderate

☐ prospect

Review Word List

☐ _____

☐ _____

☐ _____

☐ _____

☐ _____

Writing Connection

Write a brief response to each question. Use words from this lesson or previous lessons in your answer. Write your answers in complete sentences.

When have you experienced a sense of accomplishment? Describe an accomplishment and tell what it illustrates about you. Which qualities did it reveal?

_____

_____

_____

_____

_____

Think of people you respect. How do you convey your respect to them? Give specific examples to illustrate your thinking.

_____

_____

_____

_____

_____

Reflection

Think about the words you have studied in this lesson.

1. Which words did you enjoy learning? _____

2. Select one word and imagine where you will use the word. Explain the situation.

_____

_____

3. Which words do you still need help with? _____

4. Return to the Knowledge Rating Chart at the beginning of this lesson. Complete column 3. How have your responses changed?

Unit 4 Review

Activity 1 ## Make Statements and Ask Questions

Write five statements or questions about the picture. Use one or more of the vocabulary words you studied in this unit in each sentence. You may also use words from previous units. <u>Underline</u> each vocabulary word you use.

Use this chart to choose different ways to make statements.

Make an observation:	Give an opinion:
There is/There are…	I think…
I notice that…	In my opinion/From my perspective…
It seems that…	It is important/It is essential…
Ask questions:	
Who, What, When, Where?	Do you think….?
Why, How, Which?	Is it important/Is it essential….?

Examples: I think the lawyer presented a <u>coherent</u> argument.
What was the <u>justification</u> for the judge's ruling?

_____

_____

_____

_____

_____

WORD BANK

ACCOMPLISH
ADAPT
BIAS
COHERENT
CONVERT
CONVEY
DECLINE
ELEMENT
ESTABLISH
ETHICAL
EXPOSE
JUSTIFICATION
MODERATE
NEVERTHELESS
OBJECTIVE
PREDOMINANTLY
PRINCIPLE
PROSPECT
SUSTAIN
THEME

Activity 2 Puzzle

ACROSS

3. Preschool teachers are _____ women.
4. What was the _____ of the last poem you read?
8. How long did it take you to _____ to working nights?
10. Cora's essay was well organized, _____ and interesting
12. Organization is an _____ of good writing.
14. What was the _____ for raising the rent?
15. Eyesight and hearing _____ with age.
16. The movie critic had a _____ against comedies.
17. Why didn't the government _____ the spies sooner?
18. Is it _____ to discuss your boss with customers?

DOWN

1. Ted showed _____ improvement in his test scores.
2. Lou had a sprained wrist. _____, he played in the game.
3. How does the _____ of moving make you feel?
5. Did Kim _____ her goal of learning to ski?
6. No words are needed to _____ the children's excitement.
7. Our goal is to _____ sales and reduce costs.
9. Sportsmanship is a key _____ of children's sports.
11. A multiple-choice test is an _____ test.
12. Did the fire department _____ the cause of the fire?
13. When did you _____ your garage into an office?

Activity 3 Rewrite the Sentences

Use the correct forms of the vocabulary words from this unit to replace the underlined words. Underline all the vocabulary words you use.

Example: Mr. Yu _created_ a reputation as a person _not controlled by personal beliefs or feelings_ with _not extreme_ political views.
Mr. Yu <u>established</u> a reputation as an <u>objective</u> person with <u>moderate</u> political views.

1. Before Hassan could use his mother's recipe, he had to _adjust_ it by _changing_ the measurements from metric to standard.

_____

2. One _essential part_ of success is discipline, which helps a person _create and start_ routines and _continue_ effort.

_____

3. Jodie's enthusiasm began to _decrease_. _However_, she _continued_ her diet and exercise program to _meet and achieve_ her goal of losing 20 pounds.

_____

Activity 4 Complete the Paragraph

Use the correct forms of the vocabulary words from this unit. Each word is used only once.

Dolores Huerta: Woman of Social Justice

Dolores Huerta is a highly respected labor leader and civil rights activist. With César

Chávez, she _____ the United Farm Workers, a union for migrant farm

1.

workers. In the 1960s, farm workers were _____ Mexican and encountered

2.

_____ and discrimination. Their _____ for a decent

3.
4.

future were limited. Many did not earn enough to _____ a family. Dolores

5.

_____ the unhealthy working and living conditions of the farm workers.

6.

She _____ to the American public the need for _____

7.
8.

treatment of the workers. She fought for labor practices based on _____ of

9.

dignity and fairness. She _____ her goal of organizing the farm workers. The

10.

_____ of social justice defines Dolores Huerta's life.

11.

Unit 5

ultimately

integrate

inhibit

cumulative

preliminary

diminish

derive

subtle

device

subjective

neglect

fluctuate

mutual

distinction

undertake

range

thereby

integrity

suspend

substance

device subtle integrity fluctuate cumulative

preliminary derive **diminish** mutual neglect

subjective range integrate **distinction**

mutual **inhibit** suspend preliminary subtle

undertake thereby **ultimately** substance

Vocabulary Knowledge Rating Chart

How well do you know the words? Use the numbers to rate your knowledge of the vocabulary words. Follow the teacher's directions.

4 = I know the word. I know it well enough to teach it to someone else.
3 = The word is familiar. I think I know what it means.
2 = I have heard the word, but I'm not sure what it means.
1 = I don't know the word at all.

	My rating before instruction	I think the word means	My rating after instruction
device			
diminish			
distinction			
inhibit			
ultimately			

Word Meaning Chart

Complete the chart. Follow the teacher's directions.

device (noun) /dih VAHYS/

A **device** is a mechanical or electronic tool or a specific method used for a particular purpose.

EXAMPLES

People today rely on cell phones and other mobile _____.

Class Example: _____

My Example: An electronic **device** I frequently use at home or work is _____

diminish (verb) /dih MIN ish/

To **diminish** is to make or become smaller, weaker, or less important.

EXAMPLES

Using a map can _____ a driver's ability to focus on driving.

Class Example: _____

My Example: Something that **diminishes** a student's graduation prospects is _____

distinction (noun) /dih STINGK shuhn/

A **distinction** is the thing that makes someone or something different from others.

EXAMPLES

Adults must teach children the _____ between right and wrong.

Class Example: _____

My Example: One **distinction** between football and soccer is _____

inhibit (verb) /in HIB it/

To **inhibit** is to prevent or hold back from growing, developing, happening, or from doing something.

EXAMPLES

A noisy and disorganized classroom can _____ learning.

Class Example: _____

My Example: Fear can **inhibit** a person from _____

ultimately (adverb) /UHL ti mit lee/

Ultimately means in the end, after everything else.

EXAMPLES

Most people believe that digital cameras will _____ replace film cameras.

Class Example: _____

My Example: After dating for four years, Shelley and Tim **ultimately** decided to _____

Exercise 1 Use the Words

Complete each sentence. Write the correct form of the vocabulary word in the blank space.

1. The nation's supply of oil will continue to _____ unless sustainable sources of energy are developed.

2. Did the crowded parking lot _____ the firefighters' ability to get to the fire in the mall?

3. Segregation was _____ declared illegal with the passage of the Civil Rights Act of 1964.

4. Metaphors and similes are literary _____ writers use to create word pictures, or imagery.

5. Neil Armstrong has the _____ of being the first human being on the moon.

Exercise 2 Complete the Sentences

These sentences have been started for you. They are not complete. Complete them with your own words.

1. Pain may inhibit a person from _____

_____

_____

2. Besides a smoke detector, another safety device is _____

_____

_____

3. Fatigue diminishes an individual's _____

_____

_____

4. A mother's wish for her children is that they ultimately _____

_____

_____

5. An important distinction between me and _____ is _____

_____

_____

Words at Work

Circle the best answer to each multiple choice question below. Then write a brief response to the question that follows. Write your answers in complete sentences.

---

1. In two weeks, Roscoe will open a donut shop in a busy shopping mall. He wants to attract customers among the mall shoppers. Which marketing device will best help Roscoe generate new customers?

   (A) give out napkins with the shop's name   **(B)** give out balloons   **(C)** give out coupons for donuts

   Do you think Roscoe's marketing device is effective? Why or why not? _____

   _____

   _____

2. Part of Antonia's job is to explain to new employees that they are paid for five sick days and three personal necessity days each year. She explains the distinction between the two. A sick day is for illness but a personal necessity day could be for

   (A) a funeral.   **(B)** shopping for a new sofa.   **(C)** cleaning house for a party.

   What is another example that could qualify as a personal necessity day? _____

   _____

   _____

3. Trevor is attending an employment preparation class. Yesterday the instructor described behaviors that could diminish a person's prospects of getting hired. What is one of the behaviors the instructor mentioned?

   (A) dressing appropriately   **(B)** calling when late   **(C)** answering a cell phone at the interview

   What is another behavior that can diminish a person's prospect of getting a job? _____

   _____

   _____

4. Hilda works in a woman's health clinic. She knows that embarrassment can inhibit many women from returning to the clinic. Therefore, she welcomes them and makes sure they have privacy. What is another thing embarrassment may inhibit patients from doing?

   (A) reading in the waiting room   **(B)** talking honestly to the doctor   **(C)** signing a form

   How else can Hilda help patients whose embarrassment may inhibit them? _____

   _____

Word Families

Most words are part of a family of words. Study the word families on this page. Then fill in the missing words using the correct form of each word.

---

distinction *(noun)*

- distinctive *(adjective)*
  Herbs such as oregano and sage are known for their distinctive flavors.

ultimately *(adverb)*

- ultimate *(adjective)*
  The ultimate goal of the peace talks is to end the military conflict.

inhibit *(verb)*

- inhibition *(noun)*
  Many people have strong inhibitions about speaking before groups of people.

- inhibited *(adjective)*
  Some children feel inhibited about expressing themselves in front of adults.

---

1. Poisonous snakes often have _____ colors to warn other animals.

2. The school principal has the _____ responsibility for maintaining high academic standards.

3. How is a person's judgment _____ by the use of alcohol?

4. China has the _____ of being home to nearly one-fifth of the world's population.

5. One purpose of chemotherapy is the _____ of cancer cell growth.

Complete the paragraph using the correct forms of the five vocabulary words in this lesson. Each form of a word is used only once.

Men's and Women's Roles

Have the _____ between traditional male and female roles

6.

in American society _____ over the years? At one time, men had

7.

_____ about doing "women's work" such as washing dishes or doing

8.

the laundry. Hairdryers and irons were _____ used only by women.

9.

Society often _____ women from pursuing careers in fields typically

10.

reserved for men. Of course, men and women possess _____ qualities.

11.

_____, however, the individual—male or female—must decide what is

12.

appropriate for him or her.

English is spoken by diverse groups of people.

Exercise 5 What Do You Think?

Read each question and write a brief answer. Explain your answers in complete sentences.

1. Are most people able to overcome inhibitions they have developed as a result of distinctive accents—either regional or foreign?

_____

_____

_____

2. Can someone's age ultimately inhibit his or her ability to perform a job?

_____

_____

_____

3. Will a diminished reputation inhibit a political candidate's long-term prospects for winning an election?

_____

_____

_____

Exercise 6 Reading Connection

Read the following passage. Answer the questions using complete sentences.

Madam C.J. Walker

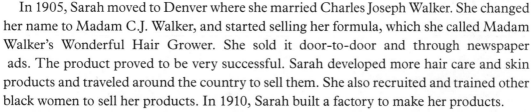

Who could have predicted that a daughter of former slaves would become the country's first African-American millionaire?

Sarah Breedlove was born in Louisiana in 1867 to a family of poor cotton field workers. By the time Sarah was seven years old, she was an orphan. She lived with her married sister and worked in the cotton fields. At 14, she got married to escape her abusive brother-in-law.

Sarah had a daughter in 1885. Her husband died two years later, and Sarah moved to St. Louis to join her four brothers who were barbers. Having almost no education, she worked in a laundry and later as a cook and housecleaner.

In the 1890s, most Americans did not have indoor plumbing, central heating, or electricity. Consequently, they did not bathe or wash their hair frequently. As a result, many people like Sarah developed scalp problems that caused hair loss. Sarah tried several products, but she ultimately developed her own formula that made her scalp healthier. It also worked for her friends. There were few hair products available for black women, so Sarah realized she had a good idea for her own business.

In 1905, Sarah moved to Denver where she married Charles Joseph Walker. She changed her name to Madam C.J. Walker, and started selling her formula, which she called Madam Walker's Wonderful Hair Grower. She sold it door-to-door and through newspaper ads. The product proved to be very successful. Sarah developed more hair care and skin products and traveled around the country to sell them. She also recruited and trained other black women to sell her products. In 1910, Sarah built a factory to make her products.

As her success grew, Sarah looked for ways to help the African-American community. She gave lectures to help women start their own businesses. She donated money to black organizations, orphanages, schools, and retirement homes. When she died in 1919, she was considered to be the country's first African American millionaire.

1. What was Madam C.J. Walker's distinction among African-Americans?

_____

_____

2. Sarah overcame conditions that could have inhibited her success. Name three of these conditions.

_____

_____

3. Has Madam C.J. Walker's relevance diminished since her death nearly 100 years ago? How is her life relevant to all people today?

_____

device subtle integrity fluctuate cumulative
preliminary derive **diminish** mutual neglect
subjective range integrate **distinction**
mutual **inhibit** suspend preliminary subtle
undertake thereby **ultimately** substance

New Word List

☐ device

☐ diminish

☐ distinction

☐ inhibit

☐ ultimately

Review Word List

☐ _____

☐ _____

☐ _____

☐ _____

☐ _____

Writing Connection

Write a brief response to each question. Use words from this lesson or previous lessons in your answer. Write your answers in complete sentences.

An inventor asks you for an idea for a useful, new device. Describe a device you would like to have. How would it be used? Who would use it?

_____

_____

_____

_____

_____

Many people living with a serious illness or disability accomplish amazing things. They do not let their situations inhibit them. On the contrary, they inspire us. Think of someone who has not allowed a disability or challenge to inhibit him or her. Why does this person have the distinction of inspiring you?

_____

_____

_____

_____

_____

Reflection

Think about the words you have studied in this lesson.

1. Which words did you enjoy learning? _____

2. Select one word and imagine where you will use the word. Explain the situation.

_____

_____

3. Which words do you still need help with? _____

4. Return to the Knowledge Rating Chart at the beginning of this lesson. Complete column 3. How have your responses changed?

derive device **integrity** fluctuate cumulative
preliminary ultimately diminish **neglect**
subjective range integrate distinction
mutual inhibit **suspend** preliminary subtle
undertake ultimately **thereby** substance

Vocabulary Knowledge Rating Chart

How well do you know the words? Use the numbers to rate your knowledge of the vocabulary words. Follow the teacher's directions.

4 = I know the word. I know it well enough to teach it to someone else.
3 = The word is familiar. I think I know what it means.
2 = I have heard the word, but I'm not sure what it means.
1 = I don't know the word at all.

	My rating before instruction	I think the word means	My rating after instruction
integrity			
neglect			
subjective			
suspend			
thereby			

Word Meaning Chart

Complete the chart. Follow the teacher's directions.

integrity *(noun)* /in TEG ri tee/

Integrity is the quality of being honest and acting according to strong moral principles.

EXAMPLES

My grandfather was a man of _____. He always kept a promise.

Class Example: _____

My Example: A person of **integrity** does not _____

neglect *(verb)* /ni GLEKT/

To **neglect** means to not give proper care or attention to someone or something, or not do something.

EXAMPLES

Katrina _____ her garden, so it was full of weeds.

Class Example: _____

My Example: John **neglected** to pay his bills, so _____

subjective *(adjective)* /suhb JEK tiv/

Subjective tells that something is based on or influenced by personal interpretations, feelings, or opinions.

EXAMPLES

Measuring pain is _____ since it varies from person to person.

Class Example: _____

My Example: Fashion is **subjective**. Another subjective topic is _____

suspend *(verb)* /suh SPEND/

To **suspend** means to stop or prevent something from continuing, usually for a short period of time.

EXAMPLES

High schools may _____ students from school for fighting.

Class Example: _____

My Example: I ask the post office to **suspend** mail delivery when _____

thereby *(adverb)* /thair BAHY/

Thereby means with the result of.

EXAMPLES

Aaron paid his traffic ticket online, _____ eliminating the need to go to court.

Class Example: _____

My Example: Martha used her coupons at the store and **thereby** _____

Exercise 1 Use the Words

Complete each sentence. Write the correct form of the vocabulary word in the blank space.

1. When an umpire makes the distinction between a strike and a ball in baseball, it is often

   a _____ call.

2. _____ is a principle of ethical behavior.

3. The newspaper article described Senator Lee's involvement in the banking scandal,

   _____ contributing to a decline in her popularity.

4. How did the police determine that the break-in occurred because an employee

   _____ to shut all the windows?

5. The Federal Drug Administration _____ sales of children's cough
   syrup until the safety of all products could be confirmed.

Exercise 2 Complete the Sentences

These sentences have been started for you. They are not complete. Complete them with your own words.

1. I took a different route home yesterday, thereby _____

   _____

   _____

2. People neglect their health by _____

   _____

3. Carlos suspended his marathon training because _____

   _____

   _____

4. A mechanic with integrity will _____

   _____

   _____

5. Teachers make subjective decisions when _____

   _____

   _____

Exercise 3 Words at Work

Circle the best answer to each multiple choice question below. Then write a brief response to the question that follows. Write your answers in complete sentences.

1. Lucas works at a large grocery store. His responsibilities include stocking shelves and cleaning floors and counters. Yesterday, he neglected to clean up a spill. What happened as a result?

   (A) A customer asked for his assistance.

   (B) A customer slipped and fell.

   (C) A customer thanked him for his help.

   What is a possible consequence when an employee neglects his or her job responsibilities?

   _____

   _____

2. The management at Westfield Medical Offices has a plan to eliminate paid parking for employees. They decided to suspend the plan because they needed more time to review it. What was a factor in their decision to suspend the plan?

   (A) numerous complaints from employees

   (B) numerous complaints from patients

   (C) numerous complaints from parking attendants

   How did employees respond when the plan was suspended? _____

   _____

3. Claudia stayed out late the night before her job interview. As a result, she overslept and did not have time to shower or get ready. Although she was on time for the interview, Claudia neglected her personal appearance and thereby

   (A) was late for the appointment.

   (B) was dressed appropriately.

   (C) was not hired.

   What did Claudia thereby learn from her experience? _____

   _____

   _____

4. Derik works at a movie theater. Last night, as he cleaned the theater, he found a wallet containing a one-hundred dollar bill and two ten-dollar bills. What did Derik do to demonstrate his integrity?

   (A) He took $100 but returned the wallet.

   (B) He returned the wallet without taking anything.

   (C) He returned the wallet but took ten dollars.

   When is a time you demonstrated your integrity? _____

   _____

Exercise 4   Word Families

Most words are part of a family of words. Study the word families on this page. Then fill in the missing words using the correct form of each word.

---

neglect *(verb)*

- neglect *(noun)*
  Parental neglect causes many problems.

- neglected *(adjective)*
  Mia cares for neglected animals.

subjective *(adjective)*

- subjectively *(adverb)*
  The manager subjectively evaluated the applicants after each interview.

suspend *(verb)*

- suspension *(noun)*
  The goalie was given a suspension.

- suspended *(adjective)*
  Doug's driver's license was suspended.

---

1. The oil company responded to the government's _____ of offshore drilling.

2. _____ areas often experience more crime than well-kept neighborhoods.

3. The coaches _____ chose the most valuable player from the team.

4. Was the officer _____ while the charges against him were investigated?

5. Because of _____, the house was not safe for people to live in.

Complete the paragraph using the correct forms of the five vocabulary words in this lesson. Each form of a word is used only once.

Teachings of Confucius

Confucius was an ancient Chinese thinker and teacher who developed a philosophy of ethical

behavior. Personal _____ is an important element of his teachings. Respect
                          6.

for elders is another. _____ of parents is never acceptable. If necessary,
                          7.

children should _____ their own plans in order to take care of their elders.
                   8.

Neighbors and other family members _____ judge children's behavior.
                                        9.

Children who _____ their responsibilities and duties are severely criticized,
                10.

and _____ have limited opportunities for success in their communities.
       11.

_____ parents feel embarrassed and disrespected. There is no exception or
   12.

_____ of these standards for anyone.
   13.

What would be the benefit of the suspension of the space program?

Exercise 5 What Do You Think?

Read each question and write a brief answer. Explain your answers in complete sentences.

1. Should the government suspend the space program, thereby increasing the money it has to support projects here on earth such as medical research or ending poverty?

   _____

   _____

   _____

2. Are there times when a person of integrity would neglect another person's needs?

   _____

   _____

   _____

3. Are the criteria for integrity subjective or objective? Are they predominantly the same for most cultures or are they different?

   _____

   _____

   _____

Reading Connection

Read the following passage. Answer the questions using complete sentences.

Protect Your Identity

Identity theft is a serious crime. It occurs when someone steals your personal information—like your Social Security number or credit card number—and uses it without your knowledge or permission. The thief pretends to be you and uses your information to buy things, rent an apartment, establish a cell phone account, or commit some other kind of crime.

The consequences for a victim of identity theft can be significant. A person's good credit could be destroyed. A victim could be denied credit for a college loan, an auto loan, or a mortgage for a house. It is possible for a victim to be accused of a crime he or she did not commit. Sometimes, it takes years to undo the damage caused by identity theft.

Nevertheless, there are ways to protect yourself. Keep in mind the following tips:

- Never give your credit card number to a stranger who calls you on the phone.
- Do not respond to emails that request personal information like your date of birth, or credit card or Social Security number.
- Do not regularly carry your passport or Social Security card with you. If you lose it, an identity thief could find it.
- Do not write your Social Security or credit card number on checks.
- When using an ATM, do not let anyone see the keypad as you enter your PIN.
- Shred credit card bills or bank statements before throwing them away.
- Request a free copy of your credit report once a year. The three major credit bureaus are Experian, Equifax, and Trans Union.

According to the U.S. government, nine million Americans are victims of identify theft every year. Therefore, protect your personal, banking, and other financial information. If you discover that you are a victim of identity theft, call the police immediately. For more information about identity theft, go to www.ftc.gov.

1. What are some possible consequences for people who neglect to protect their personal information and become victims of identity theft?

_____

_____

2. Is it necessary to suspend the use of all credit cards and ATM machines in order to avoid identity theft? Use two examples to explain your answer.

_____

_____

3. Identity theft is not a crime of violence. Nevertheless, it is serious and thereby causes people harm. How would you feel if you were a victim of identify theft? Explain why.

_____

_____

derive device **integrity** fluctuate cumulative
preliminary ultimately diminish **neglect**
subjective range integrate distinction
mutual inhibit **suspend** preliminary subtle
undertake ultimately **thereby** substance

New Word List

☐ integrity

☐ neglect

☐ subjective

☐ suspend

☐ thereby

Review Word List

☐ _____

☐ _____

☐ _____

☐ _____

☐ _____

Exercise 7 Writing Connection

Write a brief response to each question. Use words from this lesson or previous lessons in your answer. Write your answers in complete sentences.

Have you ever had to suspend plans to do something? What was the reason for the suspension of your plans? How did things ultimately end up?

_____

_____

_____

_____

_____

Should integrity be rewarded? Why or why not? Illustrate your opinions with examples.

_____

_____

_____

_____

_____

_____

Exercise 8 Reflection

Think about the words you have studied in this lesson.

1. Which words did you enjoy learning? _____

2. Select one word and imagine where you will use the word. Explain the situation.

_____

_____

3. Which words do you still need help with? _____

4. Return to the Knowledge Rating Chart at the beginning of this lesson. Complete column 3. How have your responses changed?

device integrity **cumulative** fluctuate

derive preliminary diminish undertake

subjective **integrate** suspend distinction

inhibit range preliminary subtle **mutual**

substance neglect thereby ultimately

Vocabulary Knowledge Rating Chart

How well do you know the words? Use the numbers to rate your knowledge of the vocabulary words. Follow the teacher's directions.

4 = I know the word. I know it well enough to teach it to someone else.
3 = The word is familiar. I think I know what it means.
2 = I have heard the word, but I'm not sure what it means.
1 = I don't know the word at all.

	My rating before instruction	I think the word means	My rating after instruction
cumulative			
derive			
integrate			
mutual			
substance			

Word Meaning Chart

Complete the chart. Follow the teacher's directions.

cumulative *(adjective)* /KYOO myuh luh tiv/
Cumulative tells that something increases gradually with successive additions.

EXAMPLES

For most adults, learning a new language is a long, _____ process.

Class Example: _____

My Example: A **cumulative** benefit of regular exercise is _____

derive *(verb)* /dih RAHYV/
To **derive** means to come from or to get something from another source.

EXAMPLES

The city _____ a portion of its income from traffic ticket fines.

Class Example: _____

My Example: Teachers **derive** satisfaction from students' _____

integrate *(verb)* /IN ti greyt/
To **integrate** means to bring together, combine, or blend different parts into a unified whole.

EXAMPLES

It can be difficult for older immigrants to _____ into a new culture.

Class Example: _____

My Example: A good soccer player **integrates** several skills, such as _____

mutual *(adjective)* /MYOO choo uhl/
Mutual tells that something is felt, done, or shared by two or more people.

EXAMPLES

Peace is possible only with _____ understanding and friendship among nations.

Class Example: _____

My Example: My friends and I share a **mutual** interest in _____

substance *(noun)* /SUHB stuhns/
Substance is the most important idea of what is said or written.

EXAMPLES

The essay lacked _____ because the main points were not clear or well-developed.

Class Example: _____

My Example: The **substance** of the conversation between the coach and referee was _____

Exercise 1 Use the Words

Complete each sentence. Write the correct form of the vocabulary word in the blank space.

1. The two candidates reached a _____ decision to hold a series of four debates during the campaign.

2. On her new diet, Jan lost about a pound a week. After three months, her

   _____ weight loss was 15 pounds.

3. Using the Internet to complete homework assignments allows students to

   _____ their technology, research, and writing skills.

4. What do you think was the _____ of the judge's comments to the two lawyers?

5. Many English words that begin with the letters *tele* and *ph* are _____ from Greek.

Exercise 2 Complete the Sentences

These sentences have been started for you. They are not complete. Complete them with your own words.

1. I try to integrate _____

   _____

   _____

2. After discussing the substance of the president's speech, the class concluded _____

   _____

   _____

3. A cumulative effect of several nights of insufficient sleep could be _____

   _____

   _____

4. An activity I derive pleasure from is _____

   _____

5. Teachers and students often have the mutual goal of _____

   _____

Exercise 3 Words at Work

Circle the best answer to each multiple choice question below. Then write a brief response to the question that follows. Write your answers in complete sentences.

1. Allan has been working in a nursing home as a nursing assistant for five years. The work is challenging, and the job does not pay as much as he would like. Allan says that he derives a lot of satisfaction from his job nonetheless. What is an aspect of Allan's job that might explain his attitude?

   (A) His boss asks him to work long hours.

   (B) He assists people who appreciate his help.

   (C) There are many forms to complete.

   What is an aspect of your job or school from which you derive satisfaction? _____

   _____

2. A slowdown in business forced the owners of EZ Concrete to lay off several employees. The remaining employees then had to work longer hours. Subsequently, they gave up paid vacation time. Ultimately, they had to take a five percent pay cut. What may be a cumulative effect of these cuts on the remaining employees?

   (A) They feel generous.   **(B)** They feel stressed.   **(C)** They feel biased.

   What is another possible cumulative effect of budget cuts? _____

   _____

3. At the end of his shift, Mitch asked to speak privately with his manager. During the meeting, Mitch asked his manager not to reveal to the other workers the substance of their conversation. What do you think was the substance of the conversation?

   (A) Mitch saw a coworker stealing.

   (B) Mitch has a dental appointment.

   (C) Mitch's son is graduating high school.

   Why did Mitch want the substance of the conversation to remain private? _____

   _____

4. GreenTech Company has been able to integrate a diverse group of workers from different countries and religions into a productive team. The workers all get along because they have mutual respect for their differences. How do they demonstrate their mutual respect?

   (A) They are willing to learn about each other's differences.

   (B) They never talk about their customs.

   (C) They complain about different customs.

   What is another way to demonstrate mutual respect at work or at school? _____

   _____

Word Families

Most words are part of a family of words. Study the word families on this page. Then fill in the missing words using the correct form of each word.

---

derive *(verb)*

- derivation *(noun)*
  What is the derivation of the word bikini?

mutual *(adjective)*

- mutually *(adverb)*
  The two teams mutually sponsored a summer sports camp for children.

integrate *(verb)*

- integration *(noun)*
  The integration of technology in the workplace has reduced costs and increased productivity.

- integrated *(adjective)*
  Alicia enjoys living in an integrated neighborhood because she likes diversity.

---

1. The famous scientists _____ respected each other's research.

2. What were some benefits of the _____ of women into the armed forces?

3. According to some theories, birds may be a _____ of dinosaurs.

4. An _____ information system allows schools to track student records.

5. Good parenting skills _____ love and discipline.

Complete the paragraph using the correct forms of the five vocabulary words in this lesson. Each form of a word is used only once.

What Is a Peace Treaty?

A peace treaty is a _____ agreement between two countries or

6.

governments to stop fighting. A peace treaty is often the result of a _____

7.

series of crucial discussions. These meetings may go on for months or even years. The

purpose of the discussions is to _____ each side's ideas into a

8.

solution. This successful _____ becomes the _____

9.   10.

of the peace treaty. Ultimately, peace is _____ from the

11.

_____ accepted solutions to the problems.

12.

What are the implications of integrating children with disabilities into regular classrooms?

Exercise 5 ## What Do You Think?

Read each question and write a brief answer. Explain your answers in complete sentences.

1. Are the cumulative effects positive or negative when children with disabilities are integrated into regular classrooms?

_____

_____

_____

2. Is it ever ethical to reveal the substance of a conversation about a mutual friend?

_____

_____

_____

3. Cartoons often have little or no substance, yet many people derive great pleasure from them. Is there value in spending time watching television programs that have little substance?

_____

_____

Reading Connection

Read the following passage. Answer the questions using complete sentences.

The Ancient Olympic Games

The origins of the Olympic Games can be traced to Ancient Greece almost 3,000 years ago. The Greeks were highly competitive, and sports were very important to them. They greatly admired physical fitness and mental discipline. They also believed that Zeus, their supreme god, admired these qualities in men.

Historians do not know exactly when the first Olympic Games took place. However, the first written record of an Olympic competition is from 776 BC. That event consisted of a single race called a *stadium*, a footrace of about 200 yards. The runners came from the different kingdoms that made up Ancient Greece. A man named Coroebus, a cook, won the *stadium*, thereby becoming known as the first Olympic champion.

The ancient Olympics took place in the Olympia valley, where a temple and huge statue were built to honor Zeus. Over the years, the games evolved and other sports were added, including boxing, wrestling, and chariot racing. Another sport was a footrace in which the runners wore suits of armor. Today's Olympic winners receive a gold medal. However, ancient Greek champions received a crown made of olive leaves from a sacred tree near the temple of Zeus.

The Olympic Games were so important to the Greeks that during the month of the games, fighting between different kingdoms stopped. This truce allowed athletes to travel safely to and from the Olympics.

Only men were allowed to be Olympic athletes. The athletes had to promise to observe certain standards. One standard required them to be amateurs. They had to pay their own expenses and could not receive money from someone else.

The ancient games were played every four years. They continued without interruption for almost 1,200 years. However, in 393 AD, the Roman emperor Theodosius I, a Christian, imposed a ban on the games. The games were restarted 1,500 years later, in 1896.

1. How did the Olympic Games integrate the values and beliefs of the ancient Greeks?

_____

_____

2. The various Greek kingdoms had a mutual agreement during the Olympic Games. What was the substance of this agreement?

_____

_____

3. Do you think the ancient Greeks derived only pleasure from the Olympic Games? What else do you think they derived from competing in the games?

_____

_____

device integrity **cumulative** fluctuate
derive preliminary diminish undertake
subjective **integrate** suspend distinction
inhibit range preliminary subtle **mutual**
substance neglect thereby ultimately

New Word List

☐ cumulative

☐ derive

☐ integrate

☐ mutual

☐ substance

Review Word List

☐ _____

☐ _____

☐ _____

☐ _____

☐ _____

Exercise 7 Writing Connection

**Write a brief response to each question. Use words from this lesson
or previous lessons in your answer. Write your answers in complete
sentences.**

Think of something you have done from which you derived
satisfaction. Was it volunteer work? Was it a project at school? Was
it something in your neighborhood? Explain what it was and why you
derived satisfaction from it.

_____

_____

_____

_____

_____

All learning is a cumulative process. Think of something you have
learned—speaking a new language, playing a sport, building
furniture. How was it a cumulative process for you? When did it
start? Is the process complete?

_____

_____

_____

_____

Exercise 8 Reflection

Think about the words you have studied in this lesson.

1. Which words did you enjoy learning? _____

2. Select one word and imagine where you will use the word. Explain the situation.

_____

_____

3. Which words do you still need help with? _____

4. Return to the Knowledge Rating Chart at the beginning of this lesson. Complete column 3.
   How have your responses changed?

device   integrity   cumulative   **fluctuate**

derive   **preliminary**   diminish   neglect

subjective   integrate   derive   **range**   distinction

subtle   mutual   inhibit   suspend   preliminary

thereby   ultimately   substance   **undertake**

Vocabulary Knowledge Rating Chart

How well do you know the words? Use the numbers to rate your knowledge of the vocabulary words. Follow the teacher's directions.

4 = I know the word. I know it well enough to teach it to someone else.
3 = The word is familiar. I think I know what it means.
2 = I have heard the word, but I'm not sure what it means.
1 = I don't know the word at all.

	My rating before instruction	I think the word means	My rating after instruction
fluctuate			
preliminary			
range			
subtle			
undertake			

Word Meaning Chart

Complete the chart. Follow the teacher's directions.

fluctuate *(verb)* /FLUHK choo eyt/

To **fluctuate** means to continually rise and fall, usually in an irregular pattern.

EXAMPLES

Stress and emotional upsets can cause a person's blood pressure to _____.

Class Example: _____

My Example: My test scores would **fluctuate** if _____

preliminary *(adjective)* /pri LIM uh ner ee/

Preliminary tells that something happens or is done to prepare for a main event or action.

EXAMPLES

A _____ meeting with the union took place before the contract talks.

Class Example: _____

My Example: Before surgery, the patient needed a **preliminary** _____

range *(noun)* /reynj/

Range is the extent of variation of something in number, amount, ability, experience, or other factor.

EXAMPLES

The school offers a full _____ of computer classes from beginning to advanced.

Class Example: _____

My Example: Buying a _____ is in my price **range**, but a _____ is out of my price range.

subtle *(adjective)* /SUHT l/

Subtle tells that something is not easy to notice or understand.

EXAMPLES

Aging produces _____ changes in the body and mind.

Class Example: _____

My Example: A **subtle** color I prefer is _____

undertake *(verb)* /uhn der TEYK/

To **undertake** means to take the responsibility of doing something.

EXAMPLES

The contractor needs a permit before he can _____ any work on the house.

Class Example: _____

My Example: A lawyer **undertakes** to _____

Exercise 1 Use the Words

Complete each sentence. Write the correct form of the vocabulary word in the blank space.

1. Marlene's symptoms were so _____ that it took the doctor six months to determine the cause of her problem.

2. Why was the principal asked to _____ a review of the school security procedures?

3. The _____ of services at Lincoln Family Clinic includes dental as well as medical care.

4. Interest rates for a new car loan _____ greatly from week to week.

5. The _____ investigation indicated the van was traveling westbound on 96th Street when it crossed over the eastbound lanes and hit two cars.

Exercise 2 Complete the Sentences

These sentences have been started for you. They are not complete. Complete them with your own words.

1. The range of conversation topics at the party went from _____

_____

_____

2. Before undertaking a new project, you should _____

_____

_____

3. A person's emotions may fluctuate when _____

_____

_____

4. One subtle sign of the change from winter to spring is _____

_____

_____

5. A preliminary task before painting something is _____

_____

_____

Words at Work

Circle the best answer to each multiple choice question below. Then write a brief response to the question that follows. Write your answers in complete sentences.

1. Employees at Shutter Designs must be able to read instructions and have basic math skills. Therefore, all job applicants are required to take a preliminary test after completing a job application. The results of the preliminary test will qualify an applicant for

   (A) a work schedule. **(B)** parking validation. **(C)** an interview.

   Why do you think a company gives applicants a preliminary test? _____

   _____

2. Maria is a new employee and not totally familiar with the full range of customer products. Despite this fact, she was asked to undertake the task of answering questions from Spanish-speaking customers. Why was Maria asked to undertake this additional duty?

   (A) She speaks English and   **(B)** She enjoys talking with   **(C)** She has a pleasant voice.
   Spanish.   diverse people.

   When have you been asked to undertake additional tasks at work or school? _____

   _____

   _____

3. During his interview for store manager, Omar asked the interviewer about the salary range for the manager position. What answer did he receive?

   (A) less than $40,000 a year **(B)** between $40,000 and   **(C)** more than $40,000 a year
                                      $45,000 a year

   Why do companies list salary ranges for many jobs? What is a salary range based on?

   _____

   _____

4. Tiffany gets jobs through a temporary employment agency. The number of hours she works each week often fluctuates. Therefore, her income fluctuates from month to month. What is one effect of having an income that fluctuates?

   (A) It is difficult to   **(B)** It is difficult to work.   **(C)** It is difficult to cash
   save money.   a check.

   What is another effect of having an income that fluctuates? _____

   _____

Exercise 4 | Word Families

Most words are part of a family of words. Study the word families on this page. Then fill in the missing words using the correct form of each word.

---

fluctuate *(verb)*
• fluctuation *(noun)* *Mood fluctuations may be a symptom of illness.*

range *(noun)*
• range *(verb)* *The store's diverse music selection ranged from classical to hip-hop.*

subtle *(adjective)*
• subtly *(adverb)* *The husband subtly reminded his wife about their approaching anniversary.*

undertake *(verb)*
• undertaking *(noun)* *Painting the entire house was a major undertaking.*

---

1. The movie was universally popular, so it was not a surprise to see that people in the audience

_____ from children to senior citizens.

2. A good server knows how to _____ make lunch or dinner suggestions.

3. Owen and Stella ultimately decided that adopting a child was a complex, but nevertheless

worthwhile, _____.

4. Is there a chart that provides healthy weight _____ based on height?

5. The _____ in the price of gas made it difficult to budget.

Complete the paragraph using the correct forms of the five vocabulary words in this lesson. Each form of a word is used only once.

Body Temperatures

For a healthy person, normal body temperatures can _____ throughout
6.

the day. These temperatures may _____ from a low of 96.8° in the early
7.

morning to around 100.8° in the late afternoon. The _____ are a
8.

result of changes of activity. _____ changes in activity, such as
9.

resting, can lower temperature. Fever is defined as a rise in temperature above a person's

normal _____. To find out what a normal temperature is for you,
10.

_____ to record your temperature at different times throughout the day. You
11.

will see that your body is _____ adjusting to changes inside and outside of you.
12.

Are people always prepared to undertake the responsibilities of marriage?

Exercise 5   What Do You Think?

Read each question and write a brief answer. Explain your answers in complete sentences.

1. Should a preliminary class on successful relationships be required for couples who are ready to undertake marriage?

   _____

   _____

   _____

2. Do you prefer to live in a climate with subtle changes in the seasons and temperature fluctuations or a climate with dramatic changes?

   _____

   _____

3. Do politicians' positions on issues need to fluctuate in order to sustain the support of a wide range of voters?

   _____

   _____

Reading Connection

Read the following passage. Answer the questions using complete sentences.

Cactus: A Native American Plant

Did you know that the cactus is a native "American" plant? Cacti (the plural form of cactus) grow throughout North and South America, from Canada to southern Argentina and Chile. Even though cacti are found around the world, their origin can be traced to southern Mexico or northern South America. Cacti grow predominantly in hot, dry areas, such as deserts, but they can also be found in some tropical and mountain areas.

What makes cacti so interesting? For one thing, they grow in diverse shapes and sizes. Some are short and round; others look like starfish or pincushions. Some may be tall and thin. Another fascinating feature is that all cacti produce flowers. These flowers are usually bright and colorful, lasting only for a few days. Cacti also produce fruit that may be eaten by birds, insects, animals, and even humans.

Cacti do not have wood like trees. Instead of leaves, cacti have spines (needle-like points) that are usually sharp. Spines protect the cactus and can be short, long, straight, or curved. Over millions of years, cacti developed many adaptations to allow them to live in places where it is hot and dry for long periods of time. One of these adaptations is their long roots; another adaptation is their ability to store water in their thick, tough stems.

Cacti play a role in many Native American cultures. The Aztecs in ancient Mexico named their capital city Tenochtitlan, which means "place of the sacred cactus." This is the current site of Mexico City.

Cacti grow in pots, gardens, parks, and wilderness areas. National and state parks preserve these unique plants for future generations to enjoy. Cacti continue to fascinate people.

1. What is the geographic range of cacti in the Americas?

_____

_____

_____

2. Would you describe a cactus as a plant with subtle features? Why or why not?

_____

_____

_____

3. If you decided to create a small cactus garden, what preliminary information would you like to have before undertaking this project?

_____

_____

device integrity cumulative **fluctuate**
derive **preliminary** diminish neglect
subjective integrate derive **range** distinction
subtle mutual inhibit suspend preliminary
thereby ultimately substance **undertake**

New Word List

☐ fluctuate

☐ preliminary

☐ range

☐ subtle

☐ undertake

Review Word List

☐ _____

☐ _____

☐ _____

☐ _____

☐ _____

Exercise 7 # Writing Connection

Write a brief response to each question. Use words from this lesson or previous lessons in your answer. Write your answers in complete sentences.

When undertaking a change in your life, is it more effective for you to make small, subtle changes or start with a large, dramatic change? Give an example of a time you have undertaken a change in your habits or routine.

_____

_____

_____

_____

_____

Describe your taste in fashion. Is there a range of styles you like? Do you prefer styles that give a subtle effect or ones that produce a dramatic effect? Give specific examples.

_____

_____

_____

_____

_____

Exercise 8 # Reflection

Think about the words you have studied in this lesson.

---

1. Which words did you enjoy learning? _____

2. Select one word and imagine where you will use the word. Explain the situation.

_____

_____

3. Which words do you still need help with? _____

4. Return to the Knowledge Rating Chart at the beginning of this lesson. Complete column 3. How have your responses changed?

Activity 1 Make Statements and Questions

Write five statements or questions about the picture. Use one or more of the vocabulary words you studied in this unit in each sentence. You may also use words from previous units. <u>Underline</u> each vocabulary word you use.

Use this chart to choose different ways to make statements.

Make an observation:	Give an opinion:
There is/There are...	I think...
I notice that...	In my opinion/From my perspective...
It seems that...	It is important/It is essential...
Ask questions:	
Who, What, When, Where?	Do you think....?
Why, How, Which?	Is it important/Is it essential....?

Example: It seems that the catcher <u>neglected</u> to tag the runner in time.
Baseball players <u>integrate</u> the skills of catching, throwing, and hitting a ball.
Which player has the <u>distinction</u> of scoring the most runs?

_____

_____

_____

_____

_____

WORD BANK

CUMULATIVE
DERIVE
DEVICE
DIMINISH
DISTINCTION
FLUCTUATE
INHIBIT
INTEGRATE
INTEGRITY
MUTUAL
NEGLECT
PRELIMINARY
RANGE
SUBJECTIVE
SUBSTANCE
SUBTLE
SUSPEND
THEREBY
ULTIMATELY
UNDERTAKE

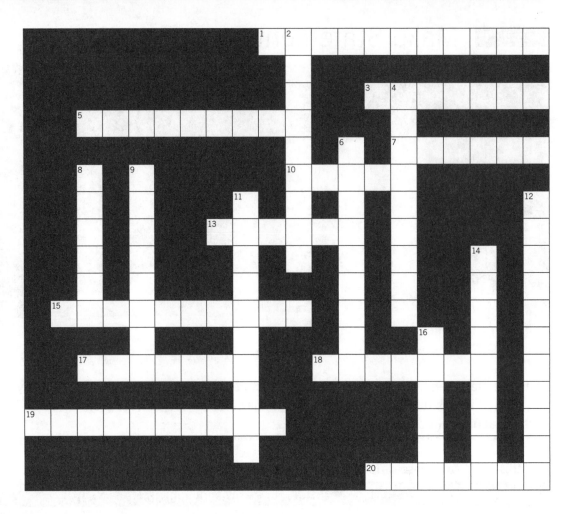

Activity 2 Puzzle

ACROSS

1. Do you understand the _____ between fact and opinion?
3. Did the weather cause Lena to _____ her travel plans?
5. What was the _____ of the speech?
7. Wilt bought an anti-theft _____ to protect his car.
10. The age _____ for this toy is 3 to 7.
13. The _____ scent of lilac was nice.
15. Who _____ won the gold medal?
17. Police patrol streets to _____ crime.
18. Did the driver _____ to fasten his seatbelt?
19. What is the _____ effect of years of exposure to the sun?
20. Bob opened the door, _____ letting the dogs out.

DOWN

2. Mother Teresa lived a life of _____.
4. Phil Cox agreed to _____ the job as head coach.
6. Mel wants to _____ graphics into his presentation.
8. Friendship requires _____ respect.
9. As the muscle heals, the pain will _____.
11. An evaluation of job performance is _____.
12. Why did the judge order a _____ hearing?
14. What causes stock prices to _____?
16. Nina did not _____ any benefit from the treatment.

Activity 3 Rewrite the Sentences

Use the correct forms of the vocabulary words from this unit to replace the underlined words. Underline all the vocabulary words you use.

Example: The *initial, preparatory* report indicated that the company was at fault because it *failed* to install the required safety *electronic equipment*.
The <u>preliminary</u> report indicated that the company was at fault because it <u>neglected</u> to install the required safety <u>devices</u>.

1. The *main point* of the sheriff's press conference was that the police have *not continued and stopped* the search for the missing hiker.

   _____

2. How long did it take the neighbors to *in the end* decide that it was in their *shared* best interests to build a fence?

   _____

3. Temperatures that *rise and fall* greatly may *prevent* the growth of many plants, but *not easily recognizable* changes rarely cause problems.

   _____

Activity 4 Complete the Paragraph

Use the correct forms of the vocabulary words from this unit. Each word is used only once.

The Nobel Prize

Alfred Nobel was a Swedish industrialist and inventor. He was a man of enormous

wealth and considerable personal _____. Before he died in
                                                          1.

1896, he _____ to use his fortune to reward great achievements
                       2.

in a _____ of subject areas. By stating his wishes in his will, he
              3.

_____ established the Nobel Prize in physics, chemistry, medicine,
         4.

literature, and peace. Barack Obama, Albert Einstein, and Mother Teresa have the

_____ of being Nobel Prize winners. The world _____
            5.   **6.**

many benefits from the _____ efforts of individuals such as these. It was
                                    7.

Nobel's hope to _____ the threat of conflict in the world.
                          8.

Prefixes and Suffixes

Prefixes

A prefix is a group of letters added to the beginning of a word. A prefix changes the meaning of the word.

The prefix **un-** means not.

ethical	unethical
reasonable	unreasonable

The prefix **in-** means not.

coherent	incoherent
valid	invalid

The prefix **pre-** means before.

qualify	prequalify

The prefix **re-** means again.

generate	regenerate
establish	reestablish
submit	resubmit

Suffixes

A suffix is a group of letters added to the end of a word. A suffix changes the part of speech.

The suffix **-able** changes a verb to an adjective.

adapt	adaptable
approach	approachable
distinguish	distinguishable
sustain	sustainable

The suffixes **-al** and **-cal** change a noun to an adjective.

hypothesis	hypothetical
origin	original
theory	theoretical

The suffixes **-ance** and **-ence** change a verb or an adjective to a noun.

coherent	coherence
dominate	dominance
exist	existence
infer	inference
maintain	maintenance
predominant	predominance

The suffixes **-er, -or,** and **-r** change a verb to a noun.

adapt	adaptor
generate	generator
illustrate	illustrator
pursue	pursuer

Suffixes (*Continued*)

A suffix is a group of letters added to the end of a word. A suffix changes the part of speech.

The suffix **-ful** changes a noun to an adjective.

neglect	neglectful

The suffixes **-ion, -sion** and **-tion** change a verb to a noun.

adapt	adaptation
anticipate	anticipation
clarify	clarification
conclude	conclusion
convert	conversion
derive	derivation
dominate	domination
eliminate	elimination
evolve	evolution
exclude	exclusion
fluctuate	fluctuation
generate	generation
illustrate	illustration
imply	implication
impose	imposition
inhibit	inhibition
integrate	integration
isolate	isolation
justify	justification
moderate	moderation
qualify	qualification
restrict	restriction
specify	specification
submit	submission
suspend	suspension

The suffix **-ity** changes an adjective to a noun.

ambiguous	ambiguity
diverse	diversity
incompatible	incompatibility
objective	objectivity
subjective	subjectivity
subtle	subtlety
valid	validity

The suffix **-ive** changes a noun to an adjective.

distinction	distinctive
extent	extensive
prospect	prospective
substance	substantive

The suffix **-ize** changes a noun to a verb.

hypothesis	hypothesize
priority	prioritize
rationale	rationalize
theory	theorize

The suffix **-ment** changes a verb to a noun.

accomplish	accomplishment
establish	establishment

Glossary/Index

Use the glossary to locate and review the vocabulary words you have learned in this book. As you move ahead in your vocabulary study, the glossary can be a useful reference.

accomplish *(v)* .... Lesson 16
to do or complete something successfully
- accomplishment (n) • accomplished (adj)

according to *(prep)* .... Lesson 2
something that is based on what has been said or reported

adapt *(v)* .... Lesson 15
to change or adjust something so it can be used for a different purpose or fit a different situation
- adaptation (n)   • adaptable (adj)

affect *(v)* .... Lesson 3
to produce an effect on or change in someone or something

ambiguous *(adj)* .... Lesson 12
having more than one possible meaning or not clear

anticipate *(v)* .... Lesson 11
to expect something to happen or be ready for something to happen
- anticipation (n)

approach *(v)* .... Lesson 7
to move closer to someone or something in distance, time, or criteria
- approach (n)

aspect *(n)* .... Lesson 11
a part of something, such as a plan, idea, or situation, that has many parts

bias *(n)* .... Lesson 13
an attitude in favor of or against a person, group, thing, or belief
- biased (adj)

characteristic *(n)* .... Lesson 5
a special feature that helps to identify a person or a thing
- characteristic (adj)
- characteristically (adv)

clarify *(v)* .... Lesson 5
to make something easier to understand by further explanation or more details
- clarification (n)

coherent *(adj)* .... Lesson 14
something that is clear, logical, and easy to understand
- coherently (adv)

conclude *(v)* .... Lesson 1
to make a decision or judgment after considering information
- conclusion (n)

consist *(v)* .... Lesson 4
to be made of or include different parts or things

context *(n)* .... Lesson 9
the situation, circumstances, or information that provides meaning and understanding of something

convert *(v)* .... Lesson 13
to change something into a different form or function, or to change a belief or opinion
- convertible (adj)   • conversion (n)

convey *(v)* .... Lesson 16
to express or communicate a message, feeling, or information with or without words

criteria *(n)* .... Lesson 1
things used to make a decision or judgment

crucial *(adj)* .... Lesson 2
extremely important and may determine success or failure

cumulative *(adj)* .... Lesson 19
increases gradually with successive additions

data *(n)* .... Lesson 6
facts, statistics, and other information used for study or analysis

decline *(v)*.................................... Lesson 15
to decrease in quantity, amount, importance, or quality
* decline (n)   * declining (adj)

derive *(v)*...................................... Lesson 19
to come from or to get something from another source
* derivation (n)

despite *(prep)*............................... Lesson 7
a relationship in which one thing does not affect or change another thing

device *(n)*..................................... Lesson 17
a mechanical or electronic tool or a specific method used for a particular purpose

diminish *(v)*.................................. Lesson 17
to make or become smaller, weaker, or less important

distinction *(n)*.............................. Lesson 17
the thing that makes someone or something different from others
* distinctive (adj)

distinguish *(v)*.............................. Lesson 8
to make someone or something different or to recognize the difference between people or things
* distinguishing (adj)

diverse *(adj)*................................ Lesson 11
different and widely varied
* diversity (n)   * diversify (v)

dominate *(v)*................................ Lesson 9
to have control or influence over someone or something
* dominance (n)   * dominant (adj)

element *(n)*................................. Lesson 16
an essential or typical part of a whole system, plan, or piece of work

eliminate *(v)*............................... Lesson 7
to remove, exclude, or get rid of something
* elimination (n)

encounter *(v)*................................ Lesson 2
to meet someone or something, usually unexpectedly
* encounter (n)

establish *(v)*................................ Lesson 14
to start or create an organization, situation, relationship, or reputation
* establishment (n)

ethical *(adj)*................................. Lesson 13
follows standards of right and wrong
* ethics (n)   * ethically (adv)

evident *(adj)*................................ Lesson 5
obvious, easily noticed
* evidently (adv)

evolve *(v)*................................... Lesson 6
to develop or change gradually over time
* evolution (n)

exclude *(v)*................................. Lesson 3
to not allow or to not include someone or something
* exclusion (n)   * excluding (prep)

exist *(v)*.................................... Lesson 4
to be alive, real, or present in a place or situation
* existence (n)   * existing (adj)

explicit *(adj)*.............................. Lesson 8
expressed in a clear, direct way
* explicitly (adv)

expose *(v)*.................................. Lesson 13
to make something known, visible, or open to possible harm
* exposure (n)

extent *(n)*.................................. Lesson 12
the size, amount, or importance of something
* extensive (adj)

factor *(n)*................................... Lesson 2
something that contributes to a result
* factor in (v)   * factor out (v)

objective *(adj)* .... Lesson 14
based on facts and not on personal feelings
or beliefs
  • objectively (adv)

origin *(n)* .... Lesson 8
where or when something started
  • originate (v)   • original (adj)
  • originally (adv)

perspective *(n)* .... Lesson 1
a particular way of thinking about something

predominantly *(adv)* .... Lesson 15
mostly or mainly
  • predominant (adj)

preliminary *(adj)* .... Lesson 20
happens before or is done to prepare for a
main event or action

principle *(n)* .... Lesson 13
a truth, rule, or belief that is the basis for
a theory, method, system, or behavior

priority *(n)* .... Lesson 4
the most important thing that needs attention
before anything else
  • prioritize (v)

prospect *(n)* .... Lesson 16
the possibility that something will happen
  • prospective (adj)

pursue *(v)* .... Lesson 10
to try to achieve something
  • pursuit (n)

qualify *(v)* .... Lesson 1
to meet necessary requirements or conditions
to do or receive something
  • qualification (n)   • qualified (adj)

range *(n)* .... Lesson 20
the extent of variation of something in
number, amount, ability, experience or
other factor
  • range (v)

rationale *(n)* .... Lesson 3
the basis, or set of reasons, for deciding or
doing something

reasonable *(adj)* .... Lesson 1
fair, appropriate, or makes sense
  • reasonably (adv)

restrict *(v)* .... Lesson 3
to put limits on or to control someone
or something
  • restriction (n)   • restricted (adj)

role *(n)* .... Lesson 7
the way someone or something is involved in
a situation
  • role model (n)

specify *(v)* .... Lesson 6
to state or identify something exactly, clearly,
or definitely
  • specified (adj)

standard *(n)* .... Lesson 10
a required level of quality, ability, or skill

subjective *(adj)* .... Lesson 18
based on or influenced by personal
interpretations, feelings, or opinions
  • subjectively (adv)

submit *(v)* .... Lesson 11
to accept someone's authority or control or to
agree to do something required or requested
  • submission (n)   • submissive (adj)

subsequent *(adj)* .... Lesson 10
comes after something else
  • subsequently (adv)

substance *(n)* .... Lesson 19
the most important ideas of what is said
or written

substantial *(adj)* .... Lesson 9
large in size, degree, or importance
  • substantially (adv)

subtle *(adj)*..............................Lesson 20
not easy to notice or understand
  • subtly (adv)

successive *(adj)*.............................Lesson 8
one after another
  • successively (adv)

suspend *(v)*..............................Lesson 18
to stop or prevent something from continuing,
usually for a short period of time
  • suspension (n)   • suspended (adj)

sustain *(v)*..............................Lesson 14
to keep something going or make it continue
or last
  • sustainable (adj)

theme *(n)*..............................Lesson 14
the main subject or idea in a piece of writing,
speech, movie, event, or decoration

theory *(n)*..............................Lesson 5
an idea of how or why something happens
or works
  • theorized (adj)

thereby *(adv)*..............................Lesson 18
with the result of

trace *(v)*..............................Lesson 8
to follow, study, or determine the history or
beginning of something

typical *(adj)*..............................Lesson 3
qualities that are usual and expected
or common
  • typically (adv)

ultimately *(adv)*..............................Lesson 17
in the end, after everything else
  • ultimate (adj)

underlying *(adj)*..............................Lesson 12
the most basic, important, or fundamental
  • underlie (v)

undertake *(v)*..............................Lesson 20
to take the responsibility to do something
  • undertaking (n)

valid *(adj)*..............................Lesson 6
legal, official, or based on truth or logic
  • validity (n)   • validate (v)

Acknowledgements

v (inset)The McGraw-Hill Companies, Inc./Jacques Cornell photographer; **v** (t)Getty Images/ Blend Images; **6** moodboard/SuperStock; **14** (l)Mikael Karlsson, (r)Mike Watson Images/Alamy; **22** Adam Crowley/Getty Images; **30** Jason Reed/Photodisc/Getty Images; **31** Courtesy Mariner Books; **34** John Moore/Getty Images; **42** (l)Getty Images/SW Productions; **42** (r)Comstock Images/Getty Images; **50** Blend Images/Getty Images; **51** Hulton Archive/Getty Images; **58** Luz Martin/Alamy; **59** Goodshoot/PunchStock; **66** AP Photo/Alden Pellett; **67** Jennifer Thermes/Getty Images; **69** Tetra images RF/Getty Images; **78** Digital Vision/PunchStock; **79** Lindsey Dues/The McGraw-Hill Companies; **86** Creatas Images/PictureQuest; **94** Yellow Dog Productions/Getty Images; **102** Glow Images/Superstock; **103** Lindsey DuesThe McGraw-Hill Companies; **105** David R. Frazier Photolibrary, Inc.; **114** Greatstock Photographic Library/ Alamy; **122** SHAWN THEW/epa/CORBIS; **130** Jean Michel Foujols/CORBIS; **131** (t)StockTrek/ Getty Images, (b)Fotosonline/Alamy; **138** Blend Images/Alamy; **140** Ron Chapple/Getty Images; **150** Flat Earth Images; **151** Madame Walker Theatre Center/Indianapolis; **158** PhotoLink/Getty Images; **166** Michael Ventura/PhotoEdit; **174** LEONARD ORTIZ/MCT/Newscom; **177** Rim Light/ PhotoLink/Getty Images.